THE FUNDAMENTALS OF COACHING AND PLAYING BASEBALL

Joe Russo

St. John's University

Don Landolphi

Brooklyn College

Allyn and Bacon

Boston • London • Toronto • Sydney • Tokyo • Singapore

Publisher: Joe Burns
Editorial Assistant: Sara Sherlock
Marketing Manager: Patricia Fossi
Editorial-Production Administrator: Donna Simons
Editorial-Production Service: Matrix Productions, Inc.
Cover Administrator: Jenny Hart
Composition and Prepress Buyer: Linda Cox
Manufacturing Buyer: Megan Cochran

Copyright © 1998 by Allyn & Bacon
A Viacom Company
160 Gould Street
Needham Heights, MA 02194

Internet: www.abacon.com
America Online: keyword: College Online

Library of Congress Cataloging-in-Publication Data

Russo, Joe
    The fundamentals of coaching and playing baseball / Joe Russo and
Don Landolphi.
      p.   cm.
    Includes index.
    ISBN 0-205-26114-0
    1. Baseball—Coaching.   2. Baseball.   I. Landolphi, Don
    II. Title.
GV875.5.R89   1997
796.357'077—dc21   97–29276
                                     CIP

Printed in the United States of America

10 9 8 7 6 5 4 3 2 1   02 01 00 99 98 97

Dedication

To Cecilia, Rosemarie, our families, and to all those people
who love the game of baseball as much as we do
and have the desire to excel as players and coaches.

CONTENTS

KEY SYMBOLS

Note: The following symbols are used to illustrate the diagrams and drills used throughout the book.

1	Pitcher
2	Catcher
3	First baseman
4	Second baseman
5	Third baseman
6	Shortstop
7	Left fielder
8	Center fielder
9	Right fielder
○	Baseball
■	Base
INF	Infielder
OF	Outfielder
R	Runner
F	Fungo hitter
S	Shagger
HC	Head coach
AC	Assistant coach
M	Manager
– – – – –	Path of thrown ball
————	Movement of player
⌇⌇⌇⌇○	Path of ground ball or fly ball

WHY YOU NEED
TO READ THIS BOOK

Baseball is a game that is played by so many, yet can frustrate so many more. We, the authors, wrote this, our second book, to be used as an asset not only to coaches but to players as well. We have tried to improve on the first book by presenting new ideas in teaching and coaching while keeping to the basics that have aided us in achieving success as teachers and coaches.

This book addresses the areas a coach and player should know when creating a *systematic approach to learning the game*. The skills required to play the game of baseball on the championship level are difficult to attain, but both the player and the coach who want to achieve that satisfaction will likely find all of the information necessary to achieve their goal in this text.

Since writing our first book, we have seen that offense has become increasingly important in achieving success but that the techniques and skills needed by a strong offensive player and team are lacking in many players. Therefore, in this book, without diminishing the importance of defense, the fundamentals that a player and coach must have to develop a strong offense are described both verbally and visually through illustrations and photos.

In the opening chapter, we provide an in-depth guide on how to set up and teach an offensive system. It is a guide to organizing a team's offensive strategy.

Chapter 2, on hitting, provides a simple step-by-step approach to aggressive hitting. When players apply all of the principles and use the numerous drills complied from top coaches across the country, they will become hitting machines. The breakdown of what it takes to be successful in the most difficult skill in all of sports is presented with solid coaching cues and illustrations.

The bunting mechanics bring forth a revitalization of a skill that many overlook and fail to incorporate into their offensive game.

Chapter 3, on baserunning, compliments the chapter on hitting by explaining how, after reaching base, a player becomes an offensive threat because of his knowledge and awareness of situations. The information in this chapter gives the coach and student the fundamentals necessary for successful baserunning at any level. Through the use of proper techniques, explained in detail, the player will become more aggressive and confident on the base paths when making turns on the bases, taking leads, stealing bases, and sliding. The content of this chapter should provide coaches with valuable insights on teaching baserunning to all players.

Chapter 4 relates to pitching mechanics and covers them simply, from A to Z. The mechanics of pitching are simplified into basic coaching and teaching terms. The essential five pitching skills, the pivot and rotation drills, and an explanation of grips will be invaluable information for coaches and players. The tips for starters and relievers allow coaches to build solid pitching routines for their staffs.

Chapter 5 gives you all of the information that a pitcher needs to know to become a complete player. The drills, contributed by many coaches from around the country, will help the pitcher, catcher, and infielders work as a cohesive unit, ready to face any situation that may arise in a game.

Chapter 6 deals not only with catching mechanics, but also with the qualities that allow the catcher to be mentally prepared to take charge of the pitching staff and the game. The art of framing is a special feature in this chapter. The checklist for catchers and the numerous drills will be ideal coaching aids to help in the development of aspiring catchers.

Chapter 7, on infield play, breaks down the infielders by position and explores all things necessary for becoming a fundamentally sound infielder. The emphasis on knowledge of game situations will be extremely helpful in the total comprehension of the game.

Chapter 8 is an in-depth study of the double play. Particular emphasis has been put on the pivots and feeds from the second baseman and shortstop. We reduce the double play to its simplest form to provide for easy execution of a complex skill.

Chapter 9 takes the fundamentals and provides extensive drills to aid in the development of outfielders. Drills on catching fly balls, fielding ground balls, throwing to bases and cutoff men, footwork, catching balls in the sun, playing caroms off fences, and communication between outfielders and infielders are musts for all coaches and players.

Chapter 10 encompasses all phases of the defensive aspects of the game. Cutoffs and relays, rundown plays, defensing the steal and double steal, and many other situations that arise during the course of the game are explained. A section of 24 fully detailed illustrations that discuss and diagram team defense in its entirety is provided.

Chapter 11 discusses how the coach's philosophy affects team selection and management. Tips on indoor practice organization and numerous drills that can be used indoors or outdoors are provided.

Chapter 12 presents an understanding of strength and conditioning for the coach and player. It emphasizes the importance of year-round conditioning. The charts and explanations of preseason, in-season, and off-season workouts are samples of what can be done in these programs. Some of the terms used in this chapter are explained further in the glossary.

The glossary provided at the back of the book offers explanations of more than two hundred terms used in this text.

With this book, we hope to assist everyone who becomes associated with playing the game of baseball. It will improve readers' knowledge and skill and assist in the development of an organizational method for teaching and coaching. We all know that errors are part of the game, but the goal is to keep the mistakes to a minimum. The drills in the book should assist in the improvement and skill development of the players and the team and, therefore, assist the coach, too.

You, the reader, must choose, from among the techniques and concepts presented the ones that will work best for you. Nothing comes easily. Championship teams are developed through the dedication of those involved—the players and coaches working together. We believe that we have compiled and supplied the necessary information to help you become a winner.

READ! LEARN! ENJOY! PLAY BALL!

ACKNOWLEDGMENTS

We acknowledge the following people for their outstanding contributions to this text.

Jack Allen, Head Coach   Drill 4.2
Tarleton State University

John Anderson, Head Coach   Drill 2.7
University of Minnesota

Bob Babb, Head Coach   Drills 3.3 and 5.4
Johns Hopkins University

Chip Baker, Assistant Coach   Drills 6.5 and 11.5
Florida State University

Duane Banks, Head Coach   Drill 4.1
University of Iowa

Andy Baylock, Head Coach   Drills 5.2 and 11.6
University of Connecticut

Bob Bennett, Head Coach   Drill 11.7
Fresno State University

Skip Bertman, Head Coach   Drills 5.1 and 11.9
Louisiana State University

Joe Carbone, Head Coach   Drills 9.1 and 9.5
Ohio University

Ed Cardieri, Head Coach   Drill 2.8
University of South Florida

Alfred Caronia, Strength and   Chapter 12
Conditioning Coach
St. John's University

Rod Delmonico, Head Coach   Drill 3.4
University of Tennessee

Ken Dugan, Head Coach Lipscomb University	Drill 2.6
Ed Flaherty, Head Coach University of Southern Maine	Drill 11.8
Howie Gershberg, Coach Anaheim Angels	Numerous contributions to the chapters on pitching
Scott Gines, Head Coach Virginia Military Institute	Drill 5.6
Mark Jackson, Head Coach University of Pittsburgh	Drill 10.2
Paul Keyes, Head Coach Virginia Commonwealth University	Drill 6.6
Jerry Kindall, Retired University of Arizona	Drill 3.2
Ray "Smoke" Laval, Head Coach Northeast Louisiana University	Drill 11.10
Bob Lowden, Head Coach Finger Lakes Community College	Drill 3.6
Mike Martin, Head Coach Florida State University	Drill 11.4
Jeff Minick, Assistant Coach University of Pittsburgh	Drill 11.3
Al Ogletree, Head Coach University of Texas Pan American	Drills 2.13 and 6.12
Bill Olson, Head Coach Omaha Northwest High School	Drills 5.5 and 6.4
Kevin O'Sullivan, Assistant Coach University of Virginia	Drill 6.7
Sam Piraro, Head Coach San Jose State University	Drill 10.1
Sonny Pittaro, Head Coach Rider University	Drill 11.1
Ron Polk, Head Coach Mississippi State University	Drill 6.18
Gary Pullins, Head Coach Brigham Young University	Drill 6.8
Rick Rembielak, Head Coach Kent State University	Drill 11.2
Mike Rikard, Assistant Coach Wake Forest University	Drill 2.9

Mike Rupcich, Assistant Coach   Drill 9.9
Fresno State University

Danny Schmitz, Head Coach   Drill 5.3
Bowling Green State University

Jack Stallings, Head Coach   Drills 3.5 and 5.13
Georgia Southern University

John Stuper, Head Coach   Drill 5.9
Yale University

Sam Suplizio, Outfield Coach   Drills 9.11 and 9.12 and outfield play
Anaheim Angels

Ray Tanner, Head Coach   Drill 2.10
North Carolina State University

Frank Torre, Retired   Drills 2.2 and 2.3
Former major league player

George Valesente, Head Coach   Drills 5.12 and 9.8
Ithaca College

Dennis Womach, Head Coach   Drill 9.10
University of Virginia

We also thank members of the Queensborough Community College baseball team for their assistance in taking the photographs for the text, and especially athletic director and baseball coach Greg Berlin and players Carlos Arce, Robert Dito, Christian Silva, and Gennaro Zaccheo.

In addition, we appreciate the comments of the reviewers of this text: Dr. Max Dobson, Oklahoma Christian University; Dr. Howard Goldman, Marist College McCann; Dr. Gregory A. Kenney, SUNY Brockport; Jeff Messer, Slippery Rock University; and Terry Petrie, University of Wisconsin—Stout.

1

STANDARD SYSTEM OF OFFENSIVE PLAY

COACH'S OFFENSIVE ROUTINE

This is a sample of an offensive routine that a coach can put together and use as a checklist for everything he wants to cover offensively. He should explain his offensive terminology and let the team know how he wants each situation handled.

Around the Horn

Go through this routine with the entire squad during training, and follow up on a similar course during the season.

Start with the Bench

Have the entire squad sit on the bench. Tell the players what to look for.

1. Be alert to all play situations so that you will know what to look for by way of signs and plays when you step into the batter's box.
2. Study the pitcher's every move to the bases and his delivery to the plate so that you will be prepared to get the proper jump to advance a base.
3. Study all of your opponents. Do the outfielders have good arms? Are they right- or left-handed throwers?
4. Does the catcher have a strong arm? Does he throw from in front of the plate in infield practice? Does he wear full gear during infield practice?

Players must master all of these points to achieve winning baseball. Being aware of these points eliminates confusion in the minds of the players and enables them to direct their attention properly at the appropriate time.

Take All Players to the On-Deck Circle.

1. As the next batter, know the position of men on bases so you can get the mask and bat out of the way in the event of a play at home. Get on the first-base side of home plate so that the runner coming from third base can see your signal to stand up or slide. It is important to be in the runner's line of vision because crowd noise may make it impossible for an oral signal to be heard.
2. Watch the pitcher to check the type of pitch he is throwing. Always be on the look-out for any movement or mannerism by the catcher, pitcher, shortstop, or second baseman that may tip off signs.
3. Be mindful of possible play situations, and be ready to take the signs when you get into the batter's box.
4. Know the ability of the hitter who follows you.

Take the Entire Squad to the Batter's Box (All are Hitters).

1. How many are out? What inning is it? What is the play situation? Is the infield in? Do we have men on first, second, or third base, or are the bases loaded? Are we ahead or behind?
2. Am I to bunt, hit and run, push the ball to right field? Will a fly ball score an important run from third base?
3. With all of the preceding points in mind, look for the sign from the coach designated to give you the sign. Do not stare at the coach and then immediately turn away after receiving the sign. This is a dead giveaway and permits opponents to steal signs. Let the coach finish his routine.

Move the Entire Squad to First Base
Detail their duties as base runners.

1. Find the ball. How many are out? Is the pitcher on the rubber? Does he have a good move? All players, when on the bench and awaiting their turn at bat, should be aware of the pitcher's move. Where are the outfielders playing the hitter? Will the ball be on his glove or throwing side?
2. Pick up the sign from the coach with your foot on the base. *Coaches should have a uniform set of signs so that all players involved take the signs at the same time.*
3. Get your lead off first base (shuffle off the base facing the pitcher by bringing the left foot to the right foot, not crossing the legs, and continuing in that motion until a comfortable lead is taken). You should never be off balance with this system.
4. The first move to second base should occur when the pitcher makes his first move to the batter (watching the feet of the pitcher is always good). Start for second base with a crossover step of the left foot. This puts you in full stride.
5. Dash and look over your left shoulder on the third step to see whether the ball has been hit. If you cannot pick up the ball, look at your third-base coach for directions.

Take All of the Players to Second Base
Let them all assume that they are base runners.

1. Size up the play situation from the base. Do not jump back and forth, getting that anxious lead. Have a definite plan in mind.

2. Ask yourself these questions: Does this team have any trick pickoff plays? What kind of move does the pitcher have to second base? Where are the outfielders positioned? What inning is it? Am I the tying or winning run? Look for signs, if any.
3. Get your lead as you did on first, facing the pitcher and while the catcher is giving his signs. There is less chance of a pickoff play then.
4. Have a comfortable lead, ready to go either way if the ball is hit or missed. Advance to third base on any ball hit toward you or behind you. Do not run into a tag at third base.
5. Go back to second base after each pitch and stand on the base, facing in such a way that you can see the pitcher, catcher, and coach, and you can also glance at the shortstop very easily.

Complete the Circuit
Take all of the players to third base.
1. What is the play situation? What is the inning? How many out? If the infield is playing in, does the coach want me to go home?
2. Tag up on all fly balls or line drives to the outfield.
3. Look for a sign to go in on a double steal. Make sure you have an understanding of the double steal. With no outs or one out, the runner on first base goes all the way to second base. With two outs, he holds up and gets caught in a rundown.

Coaches: After you have taken your squad around the bases the first week, start asking them questions so they realize that they are to know this routine and that it is very important in your organizational scheme.

TEAM OFFENSIVE STRATEGY

Hitting Routine

1. Never attempt to change the stance or style of a young player until you have seen him hit a number of times and you are solidly convinced that he needs help.
2. Encourage the player to hit good balls in the strike zone. Have him hit the ball where it is pitched.
3. Encourage the player to take a comfortable position at the plate so that he feels good and has proper balance.
4. Advise the player to use a bat that feels comfortable: a bat he can swing, not one that swings him. Check his grip.
5. Instruct the player to follow the ball closely as it approaches the hitting area and to try to wait as long as possible before committing to swing.
6. Aim to develop a smooth, level swing at the ball.
7. Tell the player to be careful of overstriding and lunging.
8. When teaching hitting, deal with each player's individual problems. Give each player as much personal attention as possible.
9. Supervise all of the hitting drills, and hold practice sessions as often as you can work them into the program.

10. Encourage young players to come to you with their hitting problems.
11. Advise your players that when in a hitting slump, they should not take the advice of too many people. This tends to confuse them more. They should go to the coach for help and go back to fundamentals.
12. Psychology plays a prominent part in hitting. Encourage players to believe in themselves and in their ability to become successful hitters and useful men in the batting order.

Bunting Routine

Sacrifice Bunt
1. Get the bat out in front of the plate with arms extended.
2. Find the most natural way to bunt, square around or angled bat.
3. Hold the bat loosely, and hit the ball near the end of the bat.
4. Always bunt a strike, except on a suicide squeeze.
5. Hold the bat at the top of the strike zone, and bunt down on the ball. Bend at the knees.
6. Try to make the first attempt perfect. Never get careless.

Push Bunt for a Base Hit
1. The right-handed hitter pushes the ball by the pitcher to make the second baseman field the ball. This is done from the hitting stance. He slides his right hand up the bat, holds the bat firmly, steps forward with the back foot, and pushes the ball toward second base.
2. A left-handed hitter drops the ball down the third-base line. His first step is with the back foot toward the pitcher, not away from the plate toward first base.

Drag Bunting
1. A right-handed hitter drops the ball down the third-base line. This is done from the hitting stance. He brings the barrel of the bat forward and down. His left hand is brought down to the left hip, and his right hand slides up to the label area of the bat. The first step is with the back foot toward first base.
2. A left-handed hitter brings the barrel end of the bat forward and down and moves the right hand to the left hip. His left hand should move up the bat, and his first step is with the left foot toward the pitcher.

Baserunning Routine

The three important phases of baserunning are: (1) stealing bases, (2) running on a batted ball from the batter's box, and (3) running after a player becomes a base runner.

Stealing Bases
1. The lead off the base is very important. Make sure there is equal distribution of weight on both feet so that you can go either way—back to the base or break for the next base. The first quick step is a crossover step, no matter which way you go.

2. Break for the next base when the pitcher makes his initial move to deliver the ball to home plate. The knack of getting the jump is the most important part of stealing bases. Study the move of every pitcher. This can be done while you are on the bench as well as when you are a baserunner. The pitcher may lean toward the plate, rock or raise his front foot too high, or look only once at the runner before delivering the ball. Any of these characteristics may be the baserunner's key to advance.

3. Slide away from the ball whenever possible.

Double Steal

1. Runners on first and third: The runner on first breaks for second as in a straight steal. The runner on third holds his lead until he sees the trajectory of the ball going over the pitcher's head; then he breaks for the plate. With no out or one out the runner on first goes all the way into second base trying to steal the base. With two outs he goes two-thirds of the way to second base and stops, getting caught in a rundown, thus giving the runner on third an opportunity to score.

2. Runners on first and second base: The runner on first has to wait for the runner on second to make his break. The runner on first must run hard all the way to second because he naturally gets a late break in this situation and a smart catcher may throw directly to second base.

3. Delayed double steal: The runner on first breaks just as the catcher is about to release the ball in throwing back to the pitcher. This can best be attempted when the shortstop and second baseman are wide and deep of second base.

Running on a Batted Ball from the Batter's Box

1. The first step out of the batter's box is with the back foot and directly toward first base.

2. Run hard to first base every time you hit the ball.

3. Touch the base at all times.

4. Make good turns around the bases. Do not break stride.

Running after a Player Becomes a Base Runner

1. Runners should always run with their heads up.

2. Always keep in mind the number of outs.

3. Get a reasonable, comfortable lead. Don't lean.

4. Know which outfielders have strong arms.

5. Rely on coaches for help if you do not see the ball.

6. Run hard on all plays.

7. Slide when in doubt. Don't get caught in between.

Sliding Routine

1. The most effective way to learn to slide is on soft grass in bare feet.

2. Place a small amount of dirt in the palm of each hand. This will prevent the jamming of your hands into the ground when you slide, eliminating injury to wrists and fingers.

3. The bent leg slide is the safest in baseball.
4. Slide on the calf of the bent leg, which must be the bottom leg.
   a. Take off from either leg, whichever is more natural, and bend that leg under.
   b. Always make contact with the base with the top leg. Keep the knee slightly bent and the heel off the ground.
5. Keep close to the ground; do not leap or jump.
6. Start your slide early. Don't slide late and jam yourself into the base. This could cause serious injury.
7. All slides can be done well with speed.
8. Learn the straight-in, hook, and pop-up slides. Learn to slide to both the right and left side.

Sliding Do's and Don'ts

Do keep eyes on the base.
Do pick up the coach when sliding into third base.
Do slide straight into home plate when the catcher is straddling the base.
Don't run with head down.
Don't slide head first into home plate.

Remember: a slide is just as good as the amount of time given to practice it.

IMPORTANT OFFENSIVE SITUATIONS (DISCUSS AND LEARN)

1. With runners on first and third bases and no outs, the batter hits a pop fly behind first base. Both runners tag up, and the runner on first breaks for second. The runner on third starts walking off. If the throw goes to second base, the runner on third breaks for home. If the throw is not made, the runner on third goes back to third, and there are now runners on second and third.
2. With runners on first and third bases and fewer than two outs, a foul fly ball is hit behind home plate. Both runners tag up, and the runner on first breaks for second. If the catcher throws to second base and there is no *cutoff man* on the mound, the runner on third breaks for the plate.

We have presented an example of an offensive standard system of play. It can become a manual for a coach and a team. It can be used as a checklist for areas to cover during the season and also as a review in the off season. A defensive standard of play should be formulated in the same way. (See Chapter 10 for some ideas.) Together these will constitute guidelines for a coach and a team.

The following chapters discuss in greater depth many of the offensive techniques presented and how to become adept at all of them.

2

THE AGGRESSIVE
APPROACH TO HITTING

To be successful, each batter must go up to home plate with an aggressive attitude and then concentrate on making contact with the ball. He must have learned two important things about himself: first, his role as a hitter, and second, the pitch and the part of the strike zone he can handle best. If the hitter is one of those rare individuals who is strong enough to hit home runs consistently, his role is that of the power hitter. Unless he is capable of hitting the ball out of the park consistently, his aim should be to hit line drives and hard ground balls, not fly balls. If he is not big and strong, he should look to spray the ball to all fields, bunt well, and get on base any way he can.

Knowing what pitch he can handle best is important so that when he is at bat, he can wait for that pitch. Smart hitters get their hits from the pitcher's mistakes. It is important for the hitter to discipline himself to swing only at pitches in the strike zone. If the pitcher can get the hitter to enlarge the strike zone, he has won the battle. The hitter is then swinging at the pitcher's pitch.

There are many different stances and styles of hitting, but all good hitters wind up in the same position when they make contact with the ball. The important thing in hitting is to be comfortable and on balance throughout the swing. Good head position, accompanied with a swing that allows the hitter to drive the ball, is the formula for successful hitting.

WHAT IS THE CONTACT SPOT?

The *contact spot* is the spot at which the bat and ball meet. Every good hitter winds up the same way: the arms are extended, the back hip is open, the barrel of the bat is about 90 degrees even with the hands, and the wrists are not broken or rolled over before contact. Weight is transferred into a braced front leg, and the back toe and knee are pointed at the pitcher with the heel of the foot off the ground. The head is looking down at the contact spot. (See Photo 2.1.)

PHOTO 2.1

To be a good hitter, the player must consistently get to the contact spot. Some hitters can take a long swing and still be consistently at the contact spot, while others must shorten their swing and become more compact. *The short compact swing is the more desirable swing.* Each hitter must learn for himself his quickness and reaction time to get to the contact spot. Once he establishes this, he has the type of swing he needs to be a good hitter.

THE MECHANICS OF HITTING

The mechanics of hitting are broken down into the following phases:

Selecting a Bat

Each player must discover for himself what type of bat is best for him. A hitter should find a bat that feels good in his hands. He should pick it up to see whether it is balanced and whether the handle feels comfortable in his hands. Remember: a bat is nothing more than an extension of the hitter's arms. The hitter should be able to swing the bat, not have the bat swing him. If a bat is too heavy, the bat head will drag behind the hands and cause the top hand to fall below the bottom hand, resulting in an uppercut swing.

Grip

The grip should be comfortable and firm, not tense and tight. The bat is gripped in the fingers rather than in the palms of the hands. A relaxed grip is essential for quickness and power. A tight grip tends to tighten up the forearm and wrist muscles, thus reducing flexibility. When the hitter swings the bat, the grip tightens automatically, providing maximum power at the right time.

Three kinds of grips are used in hitting. The first is the *regular grip,* in which the bottom hand is down at the end of the bat. The second is the *modified grip,* in which the bottom hand is about 2 or 3 inches up from the bottom. The third is the *choked grip,* in which the bottom hand is about 4 to 6 inches from the end of the bat. Whatever grip the hitter uses, the same principles apply regarding tightness and holding the bat in the fingers.

Stance

The best stance is the one that is most comfortable and keeps the hitter balanced at all times. A hitter can start from three basic positions. First is the *open stance,* in which the front foot opens the body facing the pitcher. Second is the *closed stance,* in which the front foot points more toward first base (right-handed hitter). Third is the *squared stance,* in which both feet are on an even line.

The importance of the stance lies not in how the hitter starts, but in how he winds up in the contact spot. It is suggested that the feet be shoulder width apart and that the player's body weight should be evenly distributed on the balls of the feet. The head should be stationary, with both eyes facing the pitcher. The hips and shoulders must be kept level, with the front hip and shoulder pointing toward the pitcher. Knees are slightly bent, helping the hitter to relax. A hitter can move quickly and maintain better control of his body if he starts in a relaxed position rather than in a tense one.

Many hitters like to move a bit as they are in their stance, enabling them to get some rhythm just before they swing. This is called *never starting from still.* It generally keeps the body more relaxed. Some hitters do this by swaying slightly, with their knees or hands moving back and forth until they're ready to swing. As mentioned before, the importance of the stance is to start in a comfortable position, on balance, and to wind up in the contact spot consistently.

Position of the Hands

Hands are generally held about chest high (top of the strike zone) and behind the rear foot. Each hitter makes individual adjustments from this position according to how comfortable he feels.

Where to Stand in the Batter's Box

A hitter stands in the back of the box, in front of the box, or in the middle of the box. A good starting point is to place your front foot at the front edge of home plate and then take the most comfortable stance. Place the bat out over home plate to make sure that the *sweet spot* is over the plate. This will keep you from standing too close or too far from home plate.

Stride

The *stride* is a timing mechanism that reminds the hitter to keep his body weight back. As the *stride foot* lands, the hands and body weight must remain back until the swing brings everything forward. A common fault among hitters is to stride too far, which causes them to lunge at the ball. If the hitter's body gets out in front or ahead of the swing, the hands will have a difficult time catching up. This will result in bat drag: the barrel of the bat is behind the hands, and all driving power during contact is lost. The hitter who takes a short stride has better control of his forward motion, is properly balanced, and maintains better eye contact with the ball. The longer the stride, the greater the chance of dropping the eye level. With a short stride, he can wait longer for the ball and adjust more quickly to various types of pitches. Again, the purpose of the stride is to keep the weight on the rear foot until the swing is started.

Swing

There are two different opinions on what type of swing to use. Some hitting instructors advise a slight upward swing, and some believe in a slight downward swing. Remember: the bat must be in the contact spot as the ball gets there. The shorter, more compact swing will get the hitter to the contact spot more quickly. This shortens the distance the bat has to travel.

The swing that is slightly upward is usually longer and requires that the bat travel a greater distance. Home run and power hitters usually swing in this fashion. We believe a good swing should be as level as possible. Practicing the drills at the end of this chapter will help the player to find his most comfortable type of swing.

Before the swing starts, the hands are back and at the top of the strike zone. As the swing starts, the body weight is shifted from the ball of the back foot to the ball of the front foot. The head of the bat is whipped into the contact spot with the arms extended in a "V" shape. The rear foot turns, with the knee and toes pointing toward the pitcher. This shifts the weight forward and opens the hips to let the arms come through, giving the batter full power of arms and body. The weight is then transferred to a braced front leg, with the arms extended and the wrists not yet turned over. During the swing, the front arm guides the bat, and the top hand does the snapping. The hitter hits the ball before his wrists turn over. The force of the head of the bat is what causes the wrists to turn over.

Rotation of the Hips

Along with the wrists and arms, batting power comes from rotating the hips, which moves them out of the way and lets the momentum and power of the body come forward into the swing. This is one of the most important movements in hitting. For good hip rotation, his rear foot must turn and be facing toward the pitcher. This opening of the hips brings the hands and body through to transfer the weight forward.

Follow-Through

After the hips and wrists have whipped through and the player has hit the ball, a complete follow-through is necessary. This provides power to the swing and gives distance to hits. After contact, the bat continues under its own momentum to the rear of the body.

The follow-through is from shoulder to shoulder with both the bat and the player's head. The bat handle and hands start the swing at the back shoulder and finish the follow-through at the front shoulder. The hitter's chin should be resting on the front shoulder at the start of the swing. When the swing is completed, it should be resting on the back shoulder. This will keep the hitter's head stationary and his eyes concentrating on the contact spot. The hitter should now be in perfect balance, with the body facing the direction of the ball just hit, enabling him to start toward first base with his rear foot taking the first step.

Many hitters, as soon as contact is made, make the mistake of pulling the bat toward their back shoulder, thus cutting short the follow-through. Keep the bat on the ball as long as possible. When contact is made, keep the bat head moving toward the pitcher. Begin the follow-through only after full extension of the arms has occurred and the weight has been transferred.

Zoning the Pitch

After a hitter has acquired the proper mechanics of hitting from practice, the approach becomes mental. Every hitter should learn what pitch gives him the best chance for a hit and in what part of the strike zone it lies. Every time the count is in his favor, he should look for his pitch. This is called *zoning*.

A good rule for the hitter to follow when there are no strikes is to look for a certain pitch, for example, a fast ball in the center of the plate. If he doesn't get that pitch and get it where he wants it, he takes it. He doesn't swing at a curve ball or a change-up because that is not what he was looking for. (See Figure 2.1.) When the count is one strike, the batter enlarges

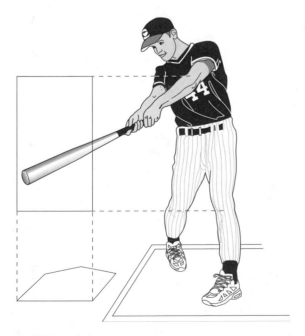

FIGURE 2.1

the strike zone a bit, and when the count goes to two strikes, the batter must protect the entire zone. Remember: if it's close enough to be called a strike, it's close enough to swing at.

One of the most important things any hitter must learn is to swing only at pitches in the strike zone. Every hitter who swings at pitches outside the strike zone gives the pitcher a much bigger target at which to throw. Don't become a chaser and allow the pitcher to enlarge the strike zone.

SOME THOUGHTS ON HITTING

One of the most important things in hitting or in any phase of baseball is practice. Practice every chance you get and work on your weaknesses, but don't forget to work on your strengths as well. As good as some hitters are, they continue to take batting drills at every opportunity. There are no shortcuts to success. Good hitters are constantly studying the opposing pitchers, searching for actions that will reveal the type of pitch to be thrown. A good hitter studies the pitcher's pattern of thought, knowing the types of pitches he throws and when he likes to throw them. A good hitter can become better and a weak one more effective. *You have to work, work, and work.*

The essentials for successful hitting are eyes, coordination, and the will to learn. Size isn't important. Comparatively small men hit the ball as far and as well as the biggest men in the game. A thorough knowledge of your hitting is important. Think about what you do when you hit a ball well; then think about times when you do not hit a ball well. Be confident, aggressive, and determined at the plate. Bear down on every pitch every time you are at the plate. Never waste a time at bat.

TIPS FOR HITTERS

- Select a bat that feels good to you, and be sure it is one you can handle. Bat control is necessary for good hitting.
- Grip the bat where you can swing it best.
- Take a comfortable and firm grip, not tense and tight.
- Learn the strike zone, and hit strikes.
- Regardless of what stance you use, be sure you can handle any pitch that is over the plate. This is *plate control,* which is necessary in good hitting.
- Make your stance a relaxed and comfortable one.
- Don't overstride or shift your weight to your front foot too soon.
- Keep your weight back and your bat in a hitting position until you start your swing.
- Keep your eye on the ball.
- Be quick with your hands.
- Hit the ball out in front of home plate.
- Don't overswing. Take a crisp, controlled cut at the ball.
- Don't open the front shoulder and front hip too early.
- Don't jerk your head off the pitch. Keep your head and eyes on the ball.
- Don't stop your swing. Follow through.
- Don't swing at bad pitches.

- When you swing, you are dangerous.
- Be confident, relaxed, determined, and aggressive at the plate. Take a good cut.
- Think, practice, and work.
- You must believe you can hit. If you don't think you can hit, you won't.

Some Reasons for Slumps

- Faults in techniques.
- Taking your eyes off the ball.
- Timing. Increase daily batting practice.
- Guessing what the pitcher will throw. Always be prepared for a fast ball.
- Swinging too hard. Meet the ball, don't kill it.
- Injury.
- Fatigue.
- Emotional upset.
- Lack of confidence.
- Listening to too many people. Speak to a hitting coach.

Hitting Drills

DRILL 2.1. Playing Pepper

Pepper games are a great way to improve eye-hand coordination and bat control. The game is played with one batter and no more than three fielders. The fielders should be 25–30 feet away from the batter. The batter should try to hit ground balls to all of the fielders and should concentrate on the mechanics of good hitting. This drill is also excellent for fielders as they work on their fielding skills.

DRILL 2.2. Swinging a Weighted Bat

This drill is used mainly in the off season to develop the muscles used in the swing. The player should use a bat that is slightly heavier than the one he usually uses during the season. He should swing the bat forty to fifty times a day and should be able to take a normal swing with the bat. If the bat is too heavy, it will prevent the player from swinging normally and put flaws in his swing.

DRILL 2.3. Swinging in Front of a Mirror

The player should stand in front of a full-length mirror and take his normal swing, watching the swing in the mirror and analyzing it. He should visualize swinging at all pitches in the strike zone, such as low inside, high outside, etc. He can use adhesive tape to put a strike zone on the mirror.

DRILL 2.4. Hitting off the Batting Tee

A *batting tee* is usually a home plate with rubber tubing attached in the middle and running straight up. Usually it can be adjusted to any height in the strike zone. The ball is placed on top of the rubber tubing.

PHOTO 2.2

A batter can work on his swing mechanics and also on a particular pitch that he has trouble hitting. The batter can hit into a hitting net using baseballs or, if he is indoors, tennis balls or Wiffle balls.

DRILL 2.5.   Soft Toss

Soft toss is done between two players. One is the hitter, and the other is the feeder. The hitter stands facing the net or fence and hits the ball into it. The feeder is on one knee facing the hitter, about 6 feet to his side. (See Photo 2.2.)

The feeder flips the ball in an underhand motion into the contact zone where the hitter swings with his normal swing. A coach can watch the hitter and make any necessary corrections or comments. This is a good drill for working on quick hands and hitting mechanics.

DRILL 2.6.   Soft Toss for Concentration

Purpose: To improve concentration—eyes on the ball.

Area Required: Small area with a net.

Equipment Needed: Old baseballs, net, bat, and home plate.

Procedure:
Step 1:   Take twenty old baseballs used for soft toss, and paint a spot the size of a quarter on fifteen of the balls. Use three different colors. Color five balls green, five red, five blue; leave five plain.

Step 2:　The person tossing the ball must cover up the color as he begins the toss so the hitter cannot tell which color is coming.

Step 3:　The hitter must call out the color of the spot on the ball as he is preparing to hit the ball into the net.

Step 4:　The individual tossing the ball must tell the hitter whether he called the color correctly.

This drill improves the hitter's concentration while making him watch the ball and work on keeping his weight back and hands in the *launching position* on balls that he must take.

DRILL 2.7.　Reverse Soft Toss

Purpose:　To teach opposite field hitting.

Area Required:　Cage, or enough room to swing a bat.

Equipment Needed:　Cage, sock net, fence, bucket of balls, and bat.

Procedure:　This drill is similar to regular soft toss except that the feeder flips the ball from approximately 3 feet behind the hitter. The ball travels across home plate on the outside third of the plate. The hitter must wait for the ball to get to the outside front part of the plate and hit the ball to the opposite field.

DRILL 2.8.　Short Screen Batting Practice

Purpose:　Develop quick hands and reaction time.

Area Required:　Batting cage or field.

Equipment Needed:　Screen, home plate, and bucket of balls.

Procedure:　The coach is behind a screen approximately 15 feet in front of home plate; the hitter is in the batter's box. The coach tosses the ball to the batter. The coach must be extremely careful to stay behind the screen. The time from the release of the ball from the coach's hand to the contact spot is 0.4 seconds, which is the same as release to contact from 60 feet 6 inches at 85 miles per hour. The batter must be very quick with the bat to hit the ball.

DRILL 2.9.　Towel Drill

Purpose:　To prevent uppercut swings and force the hitter to take a short compact route to the ball. This also eliminates long swings.

Area Required:　Can be done anywhere suitable to a swing.

Equipment Needed:　Towel, bat, balls, and a screen.

Procedure:　Place a towel under the batter's front elbow, and have him hit live pitching from 20 feet away. If the swing is correct, the towel will stay in place because the front elbow will stay in place when it is pulled down. If the batter uppercuts, the towel will fall to the ground.

THE TEAM APPROACH—BUNTING

Bunting has always been considered an important part of a team's offense. A player who can bunt effectively adds another offensive weapon to his repertoire. He can move runners along when asked to sacrifice, or he can get the team moving with a bunt for a hit. An accomplished player can keep the defense on edge when he can control his bat, show bunt, then turn around and hit away (*fake bunt and slash*).

Time must be given to bunting because it is a skill that can be learned through practice and effort. Each player must learn to execute a sacrifice bunt; one never knows when he may be called upon to bunt in a close game.

Sacrifice Bunt

Sacrifice means giving oneself up to move the runner. The sacrifice bunt is used when a batter must move a runner to the next base. The batter must make sure to bunt the ball on the ground and must not be concerned with getting a base hit. Two methods can be used in an attempt to sacrifice: the square around and the pivot in stance.

Square Around
Better coverage of the plate is attained if the bat is in fair territory when the bunt is made. The square around method allows this to happen. The batter assumes his normal stance. When he decides to bunt, he moves his rear leg up and becomes squared to the pitcher. (See Photo 2.3.) The batter's knees are flexed and his arms are extended, with the bat being held level at the top of the strike zone. The top hand slides up the bat, with the fingers on the bottom of the bat and the thumb on top. His eyes are focused on the ball, and both shoulders and hips are facing the pitcher.

Pivot in Stance
In the pivot in stance method, the batter assumes his normal stance. When the pitcher is about to release the ball, the batter pivots his body by turning his shoulders and hips square to the pitcher. (See Photo 2.4.) He accomplishes the pivot by turning on the balls of his feet to square the upper part of his body to the pitcher. The advantages of this method are that it allows the batter to fake bunt/slash and it keeps the catcher deeper behind the plate. It also allows the hitter to wait longer before he squares around.

The following bunting technique is used after the player has either used the square around or pivot in stance method. The batter tries to catch the ball with the barrel of the bat as he bunts the ball. The bat should be thought of as a glove. When it is time to bunt, the batter should attempt to catch the ball with the barrel of the bat. He should not jab or push at the ball, but should try to deaden the impact of the ball on the bat by a slight giving of the hands.

When the ball is approaching home plate, body positioning is extremely important. The hips and shoulders are square to the pitcher. The arms are relaxed and out in front of the body at the top of the strike zone. If the pitch is above the strike zone, let it go. It is very important to bunt pitches that are strikes. If the pitch is lower than the bat, go down by bending the knees. The bat must be kept level so that when the ball is bunted it will be on the

PHOTO 2.3   **PHOTO 2.4**

ground. If the bottom hand gets higher than the top hand, the chance that the ball will be popped up is much greater.

The direction of the bunt is determined by the bottom hand. If the ball is to be bunted toward third base, the bottom hand is pulled back slightly, causing the barrel of the bat to face toward third base. If the ball is to be bunted toward first base, the bottom hand is pushed slightly forward, causing the barrel of the bat to face toward first base.

Some coaches teach a slight upward tilt of the bat on contact. The barrel of the bat is slightly above the handle, giving the ball a better chance of being bunted on the ground *(angular bunting)*. This becomes a matter of preference with the bunter. The most important point to remember is to get the bunt down on the ground in fair territory. (See Photo 2.5.)

Bunting for a Base Hit

The ability to bunt for a base hit forces the defense to cheat in and open more areas to which the batter can hit the ball past the infielders. The object of the bunt is to surprise the defense and reach first first base. The hitter does not commit himself until the last second and either drags or pushes the bunt for a hit.

Right-Handed Batter Push Bunt
The ball is bunted down the first-base side of the infield. The bunt is directed toward the left side of the pitcher and toward the second baseman. The batter takes a short step with the back (right) foot and pushes the ball toward second base. The object of the bunt is to get the second baseman to field the ball just as it reaches the infield dirt. This is a very difficult play for the second baseman.

PHOTO 2.5

Left-Handed Batter Push Bunt

The batter pushes the ball toward the third-base line in this situation. He steps toward the pitcher with the back (left) foot and pushes the ball toward third base. He begins to run toward first base after making contact with the ball, not before. If he runs too soon, he will either foul the ball off or bunt it back to the pitcher. His objective should be to place the ball right along the third-base foul line or have the ball go foul.

Right-Handed Batter Drag Bunt

The batter wants to direct the ball down the third-base line. As the ball approaches home plate, the batter steps back with his right foot and shifts his weight to the left foot. The arms extend so the top of the bat is pointing toward first base and the handle of the bat is on the batter's left side, left elbow just above the hip. The batter gets out of the batter's box with his right foot leading the way. Most success is obtained with the outside pitch.

Left-Handed Batter Drag Bunt

The batter brings the barrel of the bat forward and down. He moves his right hand to his left hip, and his left hand should move up the bat. The first step should be with his left foot toward the pitcher. He makes contact with the ball and drags it with him as he starts toward first base.

Bunting Drills

DRILL 2.10.   Mass Bunting

Purpose: To improve sacrifice and base-hit bunting skills.

Area Required: Infield or area with a mound and home plate.

Equipment Needed: Pitching machine, balls, and bats.

Procedure: Have a team manager, player, or coach feed each hitter two pitches in a row for sacrifice bunts and go for at least two rounds. Keep records. Do the same with players on base-hit bunts. Allow 35–45 minutes for the drill. We have found that in this competitive drill, with all players watching, bunting improves because of the concentration levels of the bunters.

DRILL 2.11.   Bucket Drill

Purpose: To bunt the ball into the bucket.

Area Required: Infield or area with a mound and home plate.

Equipment Needed: Pitching machine, balls, bats, and buckets.

Procedure: Two buckets are placed on the infield diamond, one down the first-base line and the other down the third-base line. The batter gets ten bunts and tries to bunt the ball into the bucket. This drill makes the bunter concentrate on getting the ball into a specific area in the infield.

DRILL 2.12.   Bunting with the Top Half of the Bat Removed

Purpose: To improve concentration and bunt the ball with the lower half of the bat.

Area Required: Infield or area with a mound and home plate.

Equipment Needed: Cut-off bat and balls.

Procedure: The top half of a wooden bat is sawed off, and the lower half is used for bunting the ball. The batter should use his regular bunting technique to lay down a sacrifice bunt. With the top of the bat removed, the batter must concentrate on making contact with the ball on the bottom half of the bat. This makes his chances of bunting the ball on the ground that much greater.

DRILL 2.13.   Batting Practice

Purpose: To work on bunting techniques with live pitching before taking swings in batting practice.

Area Required: Whole field.

Equipment Needed: Everything used in batting practice.

Procedure: Before taking his regular swings during batting practice, a player bunts the ball down the first- and third-base lines, using the sacrifice bunt method. He then bunts for a base hit, using the push and drag bunt methods and uses the fake bunt/slash technique as if the first and third basemen were charging.

DRILL 2.14.   Fake Bunt/Slash

Purpose: To practice reading the movements of charging first and third basemen and using the fake bunt/slash technique.

Area Required: Whole field.

Equipment Needed: Everything used in batting practice plus some extra screens.

Procedure: Place a pitcher on the mound and a catcher in full gear behind home plate. Place infielders at their positions and a runner on first base. This simulates a sacrifice bunt situation. Place two protective screens approximately 30 feet down the first- and third-base lines on the grass. Place a protective screen in front of the pitcher.

The pitcher comes to the set position and checks the runner on first base. As the pitcher delivers the ball to home plate, the third baseman charges toward home plate and stays behind the protective screen. The first baseman does the same and stays behind the protective screen. When the batter sees the first and third basemen charge, he uses the fake bunt/slash technique to try to hit the ball past the charging fielders. He hits down on the ball because he does not want to hit the ball in the air. If the hitter feels the fielders are not charging hard enough, he can then lay down a sacrifice bunt to advance the runner.

3

BASERUNNING: PRESSURE
THE DEFENSE

The most undercoached and least understood phase of baseball, on all levels, is baserunning. Although, it is important, foot speed is not the only attribute needed by outstanding base runners. Other things that enter into the picture are craftiness, agility, reaction time, baseball sense, confidence, and daring. A baseball team that is well schooled in the fundamentals of baserunning is a team that puts pressure on the opposing players to the point that it forces them to make mistakes. A daring and aggressive team on the bases is one that is thrilling to watch and a joy to coach. It should be your objective to make your runners aggressive on the bases, to put pressure on the defense, and screw it down until your opponent, because of anxiety, makes a mistake that allows you to take the extra base and eventually score the winning run.

The ability to be a good base runner is something that can be taught. It should be your aim to work at baserunning until your players can react to given situations. The importance you place on baserunning must be stressed through long hours of drill and practice.

Field conditions such as wet, lumpy grass in the outfield, wide-open fields, astroturf, and so on, can cause the defensive team to play defensively. By being aggressive on the bases, you can force the opposing players into doing something that they are not used to doing, that is, rushing after the ball to get it back into the infield quickly, exposing themselves to potential mistakes. Whenever a mistake is made, the aggressive base runner will be ready to take the extra base.

Your own attitude as the coach largely determines how aggressive your runners will be. Your attitude must always be aggressive, constantly encouraging your runners to try to take any extra base they can get. If a runner, using good judgment, gets thrown out because of an outstanding play by the defensive team, don't chew him out. That may keep him from being as aggressive as he should be the next time he is on base. Encourage him to continue to be aggressive, even when he is thrown out. If the runner used poor judgement and is thrown out, it is your job to explain why the judgment was poor so that it can be corrected. You can accomplish this by using the baserunning drills described in this chapter.

WHERE GOOD BASERUNNING BEGINS

Baserunning begins in the dugout. Before the game, your players should be observing members of the other team in their pregame drills. Your players should be checking the infielders and outfielders as to whether they are right- or left-handed and observing their speed and quickness, arm strength, and accuracy. They should pay very close attention to the catcher on the opposing team, looking for quickness of release, arm strength, accuracy, and spot from which he throws. Is he throwing from the catcher's box behind home plate, or is he throwing from up in front of home plate? They should also watch each pitcher as he warms up to see whether he has any flaws in his delivery that will give the runners any advantage. For example, does the pitcher have a high leg kick? How does he break his hands? Is he a long- or short-armer?

The instant your batter/runner has made contact with the ball, he must concern himself with getting out of the batter's box as quickly as possible. After the swing, he must gain his balance and head directly toward first base. In leaving the batter's box, a right-handed hitter should take his first step with the back (right) foot directly toward first base. A left-handed hitter should take his first step with the left foot.

The runner should use good running form, with the body leaning slightly forward and arms pumping naturally forward and backward. You do not want him to pump his arms from side to side, because this would divert his momentum away from first base. He should take long strides and run on the balls of his feet, looking at the base, not at the ball.

The runner should touch the base with the ball of his foot on the top front portion of the base, using either foot. He should not break stride or take baby steps in order to touch the base with one particular foot. The runner should run through the base at top speed, thinking of the base as a sprinter thinks of the tape at the finish line of a race. He should start to slow down only after he has passed the base.

A common fault of many runners is that they begin to slow down before they reach the base because they assume that they are going to be out. No runner should ever assume that, and he should always touch the base. He should *never* end at the base with a jump, lunge, or slide. This would cause him to lose time and risk the chance of injury.

The only time you should allow your runner to slide into first base is when the first baseman leaves the base to take a throw. If the runner has enough time, he can slide to either side of the base to avoid a tag.

After running through the base and stopping, the runner should turn to his right, which is foul territory. By doing this, he will be sure not to give the impression that he is making an attempt to go to second base.

The runner should listen to the first-base coach while he is running. The coach will alert him if there is a wild throw and he wants him to attempt to go to second base.

TURNS

We like to teach our players two types of turns. The first is the *veer out*. This is the most common turn used by a runner approaching first base. The second is the extra base hit turn.

Veer Out

As the runner is approaching first base and he knows the ball is in the outfield, he must prepare to make the turn. When he is approximately 20–25 feet from the base, he is going to get his body under control. To do so, he must slow down slightly and veer out to the right.

The runner should be watching the front inside corner of the base. This is where he wants to touch the base. He should dip his left shoulder slightly toward the infield so that he can get his momentum going directly toward second base. As he touches the base, with either foot, he should push off hard in the direction of second base. The base can be a big help to him in getting back to full speed after he has gotten his body under control to make the turn.

There are two techniques for touching the base on the turn. If the last step before touching the base is with the left foot, the runner touches the base on the inside corner with the right foot and continues on toward second base. (See Photo 3.1.) If the last step before touching the base is with the right foot, the runner touches the base with the left foot. To get himself going toward second base in a straight line, he must throw his right hip over and bring his right arm across his body. This will get his momentum going directly to second base. (See Photo 3.2.)

PHOTO 3.1

PHOTO 3.2

Extra Base Hit Turn

The second turn we teach is used when the runner knows he has hit a ball that has a possibility of being an extra base hit. As the runner leaves the batter's box, he immediately begins to swerve to the right. He should get himself into foul territory on the grass as soon as he leaves the batter's box so that the angle on the turn will be cut down and he will not have to get his body under control as he reaches the base. He should touch the base in the manner discussed for the veer out turn.

You should instill an aggressive attitude in your players so that they are never satisfied with a single. *Every ball is a double until the defense dictates otherwise.* Once the defense returns the ball to the infield, the runner retreats to first base.

AGGRESSIVE TURN AROUND FIRST BASE

You want your runner to make an aggressive turn around first base to give the impression that he is making an attempt to go to second base. On a base hit to left field, the runner should be extremely aggressive in rounding first base. He should make the turn and go approximately 30–35 feet toward second base. If the left fielder bobbles the ball, the runner can continue on to second base. If the left fielder fields the ball cleanly and returns it to the infield, the runner then plants on his right foot and retreats to first base. He should come back to first base, watching the ball at all times.

On a ball hit to center field, the runner should still make an aggressive turn, but he must be aware that the center fielder can throw behind him.

On a ball hit to right field, the runner must be careful because now the right fielder can throw behind him to the catcher who follows the runner and covers first base. His turn should still be aggressive, but it should be shortened. The runner's technique in stopping after making the turn is to plant on the left foot. He does this so that he is facing the right fielder and can return to the base while keeping the ball in sight at all times. The runner should also listen to the first-base coach.

Runner on First Base

Now that the runner has returned safely to first base, he should listen to the coach for instructions and information. The coach should tell the runner the score, the number of outs, the game situation, and which player has the ball. The runner should never leave the base without knowing where the ball is.

The runner should look for the signal while he is on the base. This will prevent his getting picked off. When he has received the signal and has obtained all of the information from the coach, he is ready to take his lead.

The Crossover Step

Before getting into the mechanics of types of leads, it is very important that we discuss the crossover step. This is probably the most important step in baseball. It is used not only in baserunning but also in infield and outfield play.

PHOTO 3.3

PHOTO 3.4

When the runner has reached his maximum lead, he is looking at the pitcher and is in his baserunning stance. His feet are shoulder width apart. He is on the balls of his feet, and his body weight is evenly distributed.

To execute the crossover step, the runner pivots on his right foot. *He does not lift his foot.* (See Photo 3.3.) He crosses over with his left foot directly toward second base. (See Photo 3.4.) He should not straighten up and then pivot, because this would cause him to lose valuable time.

The runner can eliminate the pivot in the crossover step. By doing this, he saves time and eliminates the possibility of straightening up while pivoting. To eliminate the pivot, the runner points his right foot at a 45-degree angle toward second base. We call this *opening the front toe.* This feels a bit awkward at first, but after some practice, it becomes comfortable. As the runner is going to break for second base, he can just lean into the crossover step. As he begins to lean, he pushes off on the right foot, throws his left arm across his body toward second base, and gets himself into full stride as quickly as possible.

The first step on the crossover step should be a short one. The runner should land on the ball of his left foot, with his upper body directly over the bent front left leg. If the first step is too long, the runner will land on his heel, which will cause him to straighten up and take longer to get into full stride.

Leads

The runner should take his *lead* by shuffling off the base. By *shuffling,* we mean that he should bring one foot to the other. He should not cross his legs. He should have his knees bent, hands off the knees, weight on the balls of his feet, and he should be looking at the pitcher. He should take his lead off the back edge of the base because when he has to come back to the base, he should come back to the back edge of the base. This is the point farthest from the pitcher and also the point farthest from the first baseman's tag.

The normal lead for most runners is three or four shuffle steps off the base, approximately 12 feet. This is the *primary lead,* which is usually in the area of the cut in the infield grass. The size of the lead is determined by the quickness and agility of the individual runner.

We teach three types of leads from first base: the two-way, the one-way, and the walking lead.

The Two-Way Lead

This is the lead used by most runners. The runner has his body weight balanced so that he can go either way. If the pitcher throws to first base, the runner should pivot on his left foot, cross over with his right foot, and dive back to the outside corner of the base. If the pitcher throws to home plate and the runner is not stealing, the runner should take two or three more shuffle steps toward second base. This is his *secondary lead.* If the batter hits the ball, the runner continues toward second base. If the batter takes the pitch, the runner plants on the right foot and returns to first base.

The One-Way Lead

This lead is used early in the game when you want the pitcher to throw to first base, which gives the runners a chance to see the pitcher's pickoff move and discover any flaws in the move.

The runner should take his normal lead plus one more step. His weight should be leaning back toward first base. As soon as the pitcher makes any move, whether to first base or home plate, the first step by the runner is toward first base. If the pitcher continues to give the runner the big lead without throwing to first base, the runner is going to run on him, assuming that the pitcher doesn't like to throw to first base or that he doesn't have a good pickoff move.

The Walking Lead

This is the type of lead that all good base runners strive to achieve. A good pitcher is taught never to give a runner a walking lead. He must make the runner stop. If a pitcher gives only one look to first base, the runner can time the look and move as soon as the pitcher looks away from first base. The runner should shuffle off first base and, when the pitcher looks toward home plate, use the crossover step toward second base.

The Hit and Run

The runner's objective on the hit-and-run play is to get a good lead, but he should never get picked off in this situation. The hitter's objective is to make contact with the pitch and, if possible, hit the ball behind the runner.

The runner's technique should be as follows:

1. As the pitcher throws the ball to home plate, the runner breaks for second base.
2. On the runner's third step, he should glance over his left shoulder toward home plate. At this time, the ball should be reaching the hitting zone, and the runner can see whether the hitter has made contact with the ball. If the ball is hit on the ground, he continues to second base. If the ball is hit in the air, he plants on the right foot and hustles back to first base. If he does not see where the ball is hit, he should look immediately to the third-base coach for help.

Runner on Second Base

When the runner has reached second base, he should still be aggressive, but he must be a bit more cautious because now he is in a position to score on a base hit.

The runner is going to take his primary lead as the pitcher comes to the set position. By primary lead we mean that, if the pitcher is in the set position and the second baseman is straddling the base, the runner could get back to the base easily if the pitcher were to turn and throw to second base. In most cases, the second baseman is not straddling the base, so the runner can usually get one or two more steps in the primary lead.

As the pitcher is ready to deliver the ball to home plate, the runner should take two or three more shuffle steps toward third base. This is his secondary lead. If the hitter swings and misses the ball or takes the pitch, the runner plants on the right foot and returns to second base. If the hitter makes contact with the ball, the runner continues on toward third base.

The general rule for advancing to third base on a ground ball is that the ball must be hit behind the runner. By this we mean that the ball is hit behind the runner's left shoulder as he is reaching the maximum point of his secondary lead. The exception to this rule is when there is a left-handed pull hitter at the plate and the shortstop is shaded very close to second base. Any ball hit very hard and directly at the shortstop could result in a play at third base.

There are times when the runner can advance to third base on a ball hit in front of him:

- On a topped roller or swinging bunt that the third baseman must field.
- On a slow ground ball to the third baseman's left, which he must charge and field it on the infield grass.
- On a slow hit ball to the shortstop, when the shortstop has to charge the ball and field it in the baseline near the infield grass. The key to this play is that the runner must be able to get past the shortstop before he fields the ball. If he does this, the shortstop has his momentum going toward first base and must stop, change direction, and throw around or over the runner going to third base.
- On a ball hit into the hole at shortstop or directly over third base, when the shortstop and third baseman have to backhand the ball and come up throwing quickly. In this situation, the shortstop and third baseman do not have time to check the runner at second base. As the shortstop or third baseman releases the ball toward first base, the runner can advance to third base. The key to this play is that the runner on second base *sees white*. This means that he sees the ball leave the fielder's hand. He should not be fooled by a fake throw.

Runner on Third Base

The runner should note the position of all infielders and outfielders and be aware of the game situation. He should take a short lead in foul territory so that if he is hit by a batted ball, he will not be called out. If he is hit in fair territory, he will be called out.

As the pitcher starts his windup, the runner should begin taking a walking lead toward home plate. As the ball reaches home plate, the runner should land on his right foot. If the hitter takes the pitch or swings and misses, the runner should plant on the right foot and return to third base in fair territory. The runner should be inside the foul line so that if the catcher wants to throw to third base, he has to throw over or around him. The runner should watch the third baseman's eyes when returning to third base because they usually light up when the ball is coming toward him.

If the ball is hit, the runner continues on toward home plate, looking to the on-deck hitter for instructions to stand up or slide.

Tagging Up

A runner should tag up on all fly balls or line drives with fewer than two outs. On all fly balls or line drives to left field, center field, or right field, the runner should place his left foot on the base and watch the fielder make the catch. The runner can leave the base as soon as the ball hits any part of the fielder. On fly balls hit in foul territory down the left-field line, the runner should place his right foot on the base and watch the fielder make the catch.

STEALING SECOND BASE

A runner does not need great speed to steal a base. It helps, but it is not the most important ingredient. A base runner must be aggressive, not afraid to take a chance. He must have good powers of concentration and the ability to analyze the pitcher and catcher. Ninety percent of stolen bases are achieved because the pitcher has some flaw in his delivery that gives the runner on first base a good break.

The base runner should take his lead off the back corner of the base, in a direct line with second base. A rule of thumb for most runners is to take a lead that will give them one step and a dive back to the base. This lead may vary depending on the type of pitcher on the mound: right- or left-handed, good pickoff move or poor pickoff move, and so on. The runner should use the crossover step with the open toe when attempting to steal a base.

Tip-Offs by the Right-Handed Pitcher

- Raising the heel of the left foot: When the pitcher raises the heel of his left foot, he usually delivers the ball to home plate.
- Turning the left shoulder: When the pitcher's left shoulder moves in the direction of third base, he must then deliver the ball to home plate.

- Breaking the hands in the middle of the stretch position: Many pitchers throw to first base by breaking their hands on the way down to the belt. Once he reaches the belt, he may deliver the ball to home plate.
- One look: Many times pitchers look only once at a runner. When this happens, the runner can get a tremendous jump by breaking as soon as the pitcher turns his head.

Individual pitchers may have other tip-offs. Each player, before he becomes a runner, should study the pitcher from the dugout and try to pick up a flaw that will assist him in stealing a base.

Tip-Offs by the Left-Handed Pitcher

- Looking at the runner: If the left-handed pitcher is looking at the runner, he has a tendency to throw the ball to home plate.
- Looking at home plate: If the left-handed pitcher is looking at home plate, he has a tendency to throw to first base.
- Breaking the plane of the rubber: If the left-handed pitcher breaks the plane of the rubber with his right foot, he must deliver the ball to home plate.
- Good move to first base: If a left-handed pitcher has a very good move to first base, the runner can guess and hope that he is going to deliver the ball to home plate. When most left-handed pitchers raise their right leg, they have already decided whether to throw to home plate or first base. If the runner guesses correctly, he gets a great jump. If he is wrong and gets picked off, he should run as hard as he can all the way to second base to try to beat the throw from the first baseman.
- Toe pointing up: If the pitcher has the toe of his right foot pointing up, he usually throws to home plate.
- Toe pointing down: If the pitcher has the toe of his right foot pointing down, he usually throws to first base.

Again, there are many tip-offs, but the runner must pick out the one that will benefit him the most.

STEALING THIRD BASE

Third base is the easiest base to steal. Many teams do not hold runners close to second base; thus the runner can get a longer lead off the base. Many pitchers tend to be more automatic with a runner on second base.

The base runner should get a good primary lead and listen to the third-base coach for directions and help. A good base runner gets a walking lead off second base. It is not advisable to steal third base with a left-handed hitter at the plate or with two outs. Without a right-handed hitter in the batter's box to impede his throw, the catcher has a clear path to throw to third base. Also, never make the third out of an inning at third base.

SLIDING

Sliding is a controlled way of stopping. To execute any type of slide, the body must be relaxed. The hands and arms should be off the ground, and the force of the slide should be directed aggressively toward the base.

If you are thinking of sliding into a base, do it. Never hesitate or change your mind in the middle of a slide—this can cause serious injury. Coaches should be emphatic in their directions and commands to slide. *When in doubt, slide.*

Some reasons for sliding are to avoid a putout, to stop momentum, to avoid overrunning a base, and to avoid injury.

Types of Slides

1. Bent-leg or stand-up slide: If a player wants to get up quickly after sliding, he should use the bent-leg slide. This allows him to advance to the next base if there is an error or overthrow. The execution of the bent-leg slide is as follows:
   a. The runner approaches the base. At approximately 10 to 12 feet from the base, he begins the slide.
   b. Both feet leave the ground at about the same time, and the right leg is extended straight out toward the base. The left leg is bent under the right leg, with the instep of the left foot turned to the side so as not to catch spikes in the dirt.
   c. The runner has his hands raised and back at a 45-degree angle off the ground (sitting position). (See Photo 3.5.)
   d. The runner hits the base with the heel of the right foot and pushes up with the left leg into a standing position. This allows him to stop on the base and to advance in case of an error or overthrow.
2. Hook slide: The hook slide is used to avoid a tag and should be mastered to both sides of the base. It is executed as follows:
   a. At approximately 10 to 12 feet from the base, the runner starts his slide. The lead leg on the takeoff is the leg that hooks the base. (See Photo 3.6.)
   b. His body falls into a supine position, flat on his back and hands in the air. The instep of his lead (inside) foot contacts the base.
   c. His body and other leg continue past the base, with the toe of his inside foot maintaining contact with the base.
       The runner should watch the positioning and eyes of the fielder to determine the direction in which to slide to evade the tag. He should also listen to the directions of the coach.
3. Straight-in slide: This slide is very much like the bent-leg slide and should be used when the runner wants to get to the base as quickly as possible. When the play is going to be close, the runner should go straight in and not use the hook slide, which makes him slide a longer distance to the base.
4. Head-first slide or dive: Many players have taken to the head-first slide because it is faster, but it is also more dangerous. The runner can take off from approximately 15 feet from the base. He should be running at full speed and should glide into the head-first slide. He should not jump or bellywhop into the slide. The runner's hands and

PHOTO 3.5

PHOTO 3.6

arms should be extended and relaxed. His chest and abdomen should take the brunt of the slide. His thighs should be slightly off the ground, and his hands should grab the base, with wrists at a 45-degree angle so as not to jam the fingers into the base.

Teaching Sliding

All players should be taught to slide. Each player should be able to master at least one slide completely and should try to master all of them. The players must first learn to slide, not jump.

Break sliding down into stages. Have the players remove their spikes and wear sweat pants and sliding pads.

Stage 1: sit down through the slide
Have the players sit on the ground, in the position of each slide in sequence.

Stage 2: fall into slide
After they have sat through the slide, have the players stand up and fall into the position of the slide.

Stage 3: slow motion
Place a movable base on a soft, level, grassy area in the outfield. You can wet the area down to allow the players to slide farther and easier.

Stage 4: full speed
As players become more adept at sliding, follow the procedure for slow motion. At this point, you can have contests with the players to see who can slide the longest distance, who has the best technique, and so on.

TIPS FOR SLIDERS

- When leading off a base, pick up dirt in both hands. This serves as a reminder to keep hands and arms off the ground and helps avoid wrist jamming and slide burns of the hands and arms. Wearing batting gloves on both hands accomplishes the same result.
- When sliding, keep your spikes turned to the side or up to avoid catching them in the ground.
- The takeoff point should be between 10 and 15 feet from the base, according to the type of slide required.
- Watch the eyes and positioning of the fielder to determine the direction in which to slide.
- Listen to the coach and watch his signals for instructions on the direction in which to slide.
- Be ready to stand up and advance on an overthrow.
- Beware of the decoy and quick tag.
- Take-out slides are meant to harass—never to injure.
- When in doubt, slide.
- Never change your mind in the middle of a slide.

Baserunning Drills

DRILL 3.1.   All-Purpose Baserunning Drill

This drill is used to practice baserunning techniques and also to improve general conditioning of players. The drill begins with the whole team, pitchers included, lined up behind home plate facing first base.

Run from home to first base: Each player steps into the batter's box, right-handed hitters in the right-hand box, left-hand hitters in the left-hand box. The first player steps into the box and takes a simulated swing. He leaves the box by stepping toward first base with his back foot. He then uses good running form as he runs along the foul line toward first base. As he approaches first base, he touches the top front portion of the base with either foot. He should not break stride as he runs through the base. He should run to a point 15–20 feet past the base, turn to his right into foul territory, and then jog back toward home plate. Each player on the team follows the same routine.

Round first base and come back, watching the ball: The first player steps into the batter's box, swings, and runs to first base. As he approaches first base, he uses the veer-out turn, touches the base, and makes an aggressive turn. He then plants on the right foot and comes back to the base, watching the ball.

Round first base, hesitate, and go to second base: The first player steps into the batter's box, swings, and runs to first base. As he approaches first base, he uses the veer-out turn, touches the base, and makes an aggressive turn toward second base. He plants on the right foot and retreats toward first base, watching the ball at all times. As he takes his third step toward first base, he plants on the left foot and heads toward second base. This part of the drill simulates an outfielder's bobbling the ball or overthrowing the cutoff man.

Lead off first base: All players line up by the first-base coaching box. The first player takes his lead. He uses the crossover step and simulates stealing second base. When he is about 20 feet from second base, he glances over his left shoulder and looks to the third-base coach for a signal to continue to third base or stop at second base. This also gives the third-base coach a chance to practice giving signs to the runners.

Lead off second base and score on a base hit: The players line up behind second base, and the first player takes his primary lead. He then takes his secondary lead and breaks toward third-base. As he approaches third base, he should listen to the third-base coach for a verbal signal and watch him for a visual sign as to whether he should continue to home plate or stop at third base.

Tag up at third base: All players line up behind third base. Each player takes his walking lead in foul territory, lands on his right foot, and assumes a fly ball has been hit to the outfield. He plants on the right foot and returns to third base. Using the proper technique, the runner tags up and runs at full speed through home plate.

Run to second base on a double: All players line up at home plate again. The first player, using the extra base hit turn, runs hard all the way to second base.

Run to third base on a triple: This is the same procedure as running to second base on a double.

Run from home to home: This is the same procedure as running to second and third bases.

DRILL 3.2.   Baserunning and Catching Drill

Purpose: To pit the base runners against the catchers in stealing second base. After completing the conditioning and exercise program at the start of every practice, start this competition.

Procedure:

1. Measure and mark off two lanes of 90 feet about 10 or 20 feet back off the base-line from first to second base. Mark a line 12 feet out from the base to indicate a safe lead and another line 15 feet out to indicate an aggressive base stealing lead.
2. Have two loose bases from which the pair of runners take their lead out to the 12-foot line, each with his right foot on the 12-foot line.
3. Have the runners paired off according to speed, faster runners together to challenge each other.
4. Have the catchers in full gear, with a hitter at the plate ready to swing and miss at the ball to simulate a game situation.
5. Station on the mound a right-handed pitcher who is warmed up and ready to throw at game speed.
6. Place two coaches with stopwatches at second base and a recorder at second base to write down times.
7. Place a coach with a stopwatch at home plate to time and record *glove-to-glove times* (the time elapsed from the pitch's hitting the catcher's glove, the throw to the second baseman's glove, and the ball's hitting the second baseman's glove).
8. Position a large screen behind second base to protect the runners from wild throws by the catcher and also to protect the timers.

The drill begins when two runners take their 12-foot lead as the right-handed pitcher stretches and comes to the set position. If the pitcher attempts a pickoff, the runners must get back to first base or have a penalty mark assessed against them by the recorder. When the pitcher makes his move to the plate, the runners pivot on the balls of their feet, use the crossover step, and sprint toward second base in an attempt to steal. The runners must take two strides and then look to the plate to see whether the ball has been hit or missed, is a passed ball, or is a wild pitch. If they fail to look, a penalty mark is assessed.

The runners sprint across the line at second base. No sliding is allowed. The timers start the watches at the pitcher's first move and stop the watches as the runners cross the line.

Each player runs a second time each day in the other lane, to accommodate any human error on the watches. One coach works with and times the catchers while the remaining coaches work with the runners.

Players run from a 12-foot lead for at least one week, getting ten timed runs. The next week they run from a 15-foot lead to emphasize the significant difference in time (approximately 0.2 second).

DRILL 3.3. Johns Hopkins University Baserunning

Purpose: To work on hit and run, running at second base, and anticipating a ground ball.

Area Required: Full field.

Equipment Needed: Bats, balls, and helmets.

Procedure: Divide hitters into four groups. Group 1 goes to first base, Group 2 goes to second base, Group 3 goes to third base, and Group 4 goes to home plate.

1. The coach throws batting practice.
2. The hitter employs a hit-and-run swing, trying to hit the ball on the ground and to the right side.
3. The runner at first base breaks with the pitch, watching the ball as in hit and run.
4. The runner at second base plays as if he were the only runner on base.
5. The runner on third base anticipates a ground ball and breaks at the crack of the bat.
6. Each player then advances to the back of the line at the next base.

DRILL 3.4. Run Drills

Purpose: To teach the proper fundamentals and obtain the maximum number of repetitions in a short period of time.

Area Required: Infield.

Equipment Needed: Baseballs and helmets.

Procedure:
1. Have your outfielders, extra catchers, and infielders put a helmet on and occupy a base.
2. Line up the pitchers in foul territory between home plate and first base.
3. Have the pitchers go one at a time.
4. Position a coach behind the mound with baseballs.
5. Have the infielders take their respective positions, with two at each position, if possible.
6. The coach starts the drill at first base with a throw to the first baseman.
7. He runs the runner toward second base, hoping to get him out with either one or no throws.
8. The coach then runs the drill at second and third bases. The drill should last about five minutes.

DRILL 3.5.   Watch Ball—Base—Ball Drill

Purpose: To teach baserunners to make their own decisions.

Area Required: Full Field.

Equipment Needed: Fungo bat and balls, helmets for runners.

Procedure: The runner on first base takes his secondary lead and breaks for second base. The fungo hitter hits the ball to left field. The runner looks at the ball, then at second base as he approaches and tags it, and then at the left fielder fielding the ball; he makes his decision about advancing to third base. The same drill can be used with a hit to center and right field, using a coach at third base to help the runner make his decision.

DRILL 3.6.   Multiple Baserunning Drill

Purpose: To work on a variety of baserunning techniques in a short period of time.

Area Required: 90-foot square.

Equipment Needed: Three bases and a home plate.

Procedure: Divide the team into an equal number of players at each base. Have a pitcher or coach on the mound, working from the stretch position. Have a coach at third base.

The pitcher or coach goes through the motion of throwing to the hitter or to a base, and the runners react. If the pitcher throws to home plate, the hitter swings and works on getting out of the box and down the first-base line, running straight through the base or making a predetermined turn.

The runner at first base can work on hit-and-run fundamentals, straight and delayed steals, and so on, and then pick up the coach at third base for a sign to stay or advance.

The runner at second base takes his secondary lead, breaks for third as if the ball were hit behind him on the ground, and picks up the coach to see whether he should score.

The runner at third base tags up and scores.

4

FUNDAMENTAL FOUNDATIONS FOR PITCHING

DEVELOPING PITCHING MECHANICS

You have often heard that pitching is 70 percent to 80 percent of the game. There is little doubt that a team's success depends on the success of the pitching staff. Your pitchers must be in great physical condition and mentally ready to pitch a good ball game. No other team game is dominated by one individual as much as baseball is by its pitchers. If your team does not possess sound pitching, the members are in for a long season.

Make every possible effort to develop good pitching, and ensure it with great defensive play. The skill of your pitchers and their success depend to a large degree on their mental equipment. Like most human achievements, success in pitching is determined mainly by what is above the eyebrows. Young pitchers must be able to think and should be equipped mentally with these attributes: determination, confidence, desire to win, poise, balance, and great courage. Each of these qualities will be required in every game in which they play. Although this may be true for all players, it is particularly true for baseball pitchers.

You will spend hours with your pitchers. They carry your defensive load, and they need all the help you can give them. Despite this, do not overcoach them to the extent they become confused by instruction.

Pitchers usually fall into three categories: really hard throwers with good stuff, really good control pitchers who have the ability to change speeds and get the curveball over when behind the hitter, and pitchers who resort to freak pitches and trick deliveries. Good pitchers simply get hitters out, and weak pitchers are usually beaten all the time.

The greatest physical asset a pitcher can possess is *control*. He may have a great repertoire of pitches, but unless he has the ability to control the pitches, his chances of becoming a good pitcher are very limited.

Coordination of *arm and body* movement is essential. When a pitcher's arm and body are forced to work independently of one another, he loses all of his mechanical advantage, and the arm bears the brunt of the effort. Your goal as a coach is to help your pitcher develop

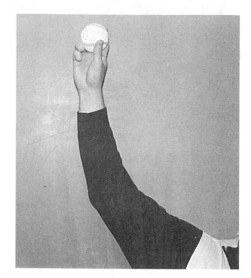

PHOTO 4.1   **PHOTO 4.2**

a good fastball and breaking pitch, along with control. This is generally the result of a smooth, coordinated delivery, in which the pitcher maintains his balance and allows his arm and body to work together.

Successful pitchers have different styles of delivery. However, balance, hand speed, grip and ball rotation, weight retention, and a good follow-through are essential in all pitching styles. A pitcher must be comfortable when throwing. When he finds the style best suited for him, he must work to perfect it. Only through constant practice can any pitcher hope to acquire a *groove* that will allow him to be in control of his pitches at all times.

General styles of pitching fall into the following angle categories: Pitchers who throw down at the hitter generally use an overhand or three-quarter angle. This permits a pitcher to use his full arm leverage and allows him to throw the ball on a vertical plane. It breaks his curveball down and causes his fastball to ride up, up and in, or down and in. If the angle of the arm gets farther away from the body than three-quarters, it will be difficult to break the curveball down, forcing the pitcher to throw a *slurve* or *slider* as his breaking pitch.

Young pitchers must find the most comfortable way of throwing and then apply the basic mechanics that will allow them to become as successful as possible. To find the most comfortable angle of delivery, position the pitcher in the outfield approximately 200 feet from home plate. The coach should be approximately 30 feet from the pitcher and roll a ball directly toward him.

The pitcher should field the ball with two hands as an infielder would and throw the ball as quickly and as hard as he can to a catcher at home plate. This allows both the coach and the pitcher to discover the most comfortable arm angle in which the pitcher can obtain power in his throw. For example, a three-quarter arm angle pitcher throws from the three-quarter arm position. (See Photo 4.1.) An overhand pitcher throws directly over the top. (See Photo 4.2.) Other pitchers throw sidearm. (See Photo 4.3.)

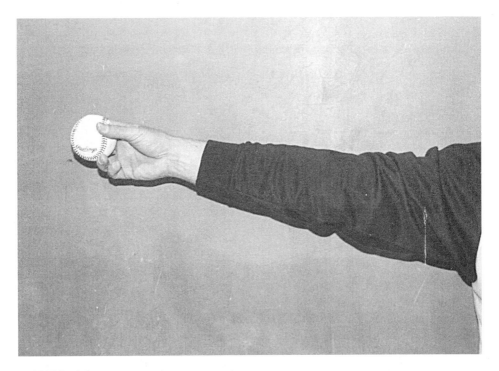

PHOTO 4.3

THE ESSENTIAL FIVE PITCHING SKILLS

Balance, hand speed, ball rotation and grip, weight retention, and follow-through are called the *Essential Five Pitching Skills*. The value of concentrating on the essential five is that it allows the coach and the pitcher to see what points need to be understood and what points may be used as cues and checkpoints in the learning process.

Balance

A pitcher must maintain his balance throughout his delivery. A loss of balance generally causes the pitcher to rush his body, resulting in uncoordinated arm and body movement. A loss of balance can also throw the pitcher's head, shoulders, and hips off the target, making it difficult for him to control his pitches. When the pitcher comes to the pivot position, he should be able to pause and look at the catcher's glove, with his stride leg up and his lead shoulder and hip pointed toward the batter, without falling forward or off to either side. A good way to check is to place the pitcher on his pivot foot and see whether he can hold his balance for a few seconds while standing on a flat surface or floor. When balancing on the floor is mastered, advance to the following drill.

Balance Drill

DRILL 4.1.   4 × 4 Balance Drill for Pitchers

Purpose: To teach pitchers to maintain their balance before throwing to home plate.

Area Required: Enough room for the pitcher to go through his pitching delivery.

Equipment Needed: 4 × 4 wooden board, mirror, and glove.

Procedure: A pitcher uses the 4 × 4 board as the pitching rubber. As he lifts his leg, he must balance on top of the wood. Maintaining his balance, he continues and finishes his delivery.

This drill should be used from the windup and the stretch positions. The pitcher should keep his weight on the inside of his pivot foot. The pitcher follows the delivery in the mirror and checks for any flaws in his mechanics.

Hand Speed

Hand speed is the time elapsed from the moment the throwing wrist begins to go forward until the ball is released. The greater the hand speed, the more velocity and spin the ball has. Hand speed is increased as the pitching elbow is raised, because of the fuller arm extension. The more the arm is extended, the more hand speed is obtained. Breaking the hands from the pivot vertically and above the belt helps straighten the pitching arm as it comes out of the glove, and it also increases the momentum going into the power release areas. A full wrist snap and follow-through, along with a good grip in which the pitcher does not choke the ball, also increases the hand speed.

Ball Rotation and Grip

The way the ball rotates controls the direction in which it moves. If a fastball has backspin, it will rise. If a ball has overspin (a curveball), it will drop. Finger pressure can cause the ball to move in the direction the pitcher chooses. Applying more pressure on the index finger and turning the ball over slightly gives him a sinking fastball. Holding the ball slightly off center and allowing the middle finger to push the ball off the inside of the index finger makes the ball slide.

Have your pitcher experiment with different grips to see which one gives him the best movement and control of the ball. In most cases, the top fingers and thumb should be on a seam to get better spin on the ball. It is also important that the ball not be choked too far back in the palm because this retards the wrist snap. An exception to this is when the pitcher wants to throw a change-up.

Weight Retention

Rushing the body, that is, shifting the body weight forward too soon, can be one of the biggest problems a pitcher faces. He must hold back or retain his body weight long enough for the pitching arm to bring it forward. Check to ensure that when the stride leg lands, the pitching arm is up, with the wrist loose and the palm down. The upper body should not lean forward until the throwing arm comes through, opening the front shoulder and bringing the body behind the pitch.

When the body weight goes forward before the arm does, the arm usually takes a short-cut to catch up. This results in short-arming the ball (dropped elbow), which causes loss of hand speed and reduces the downward flight of the ball. Rushing can also cause the body to get too far ahead of the arm. This places all of the strain on the arm.

Follow-Through

Follow-through is important for speed and control and allows the pitcher to be in good fielding position. The body weight should be over a bent front knee and on the ball of the foot. The pitching arm should snap straight across the chest to a position alongside the front knee. This pitching against the resistance of the front leg gives the pitch its final snap. As the ball is released, the glove hand should remain close to the side of the body, with the palm facing out. The rear leg is carried forward and planted a comfortable distance to the side and a little ahead of the striding leg. This puts the pitcher in a square position, facing the batter and ready for any ball hit back at him.

GRIPS

The best grip is the one that feels comfortable and gives the most movement. In most cases, the middle and index fingers, along with the thumb, rest on a seam of the ball. This allows better control of the ball and produces more spin. The middle and index fingers are slightly hooked around the ball about $\frac{1}{8}$ inch apart from one another. The thumb is straight and underneath the ball in the middle of the two top fingers. The rest of the fingers are alongside the ball. The three pressure points are the index and middle fingertips and the thumb joint. The ball should be held fairly loosely not in a choked position, which would make the muscles in the wrist and forearm tense.

The Fastball

There are two ways to grip the fastball: with the seams and across the seams. The pitcher should hold the ball as far out in the front portion of the index and middle fingers as possible while still maintaining comfort and the ability to control the ball. He should try to achieve strong pressure on the fingertips while he snaps his wrist down to create the spin that causes the ball to move.

Holding the Ball across the Seams (Four-Seam Rotation)

When gripping the ball across the seams, the two top fingers are at a point where the seams are farthest apart. The thumb is underneath the ball, resting on the bottom seam. When the ball is released with a vigorous wrist snap, it creates backspin on the ball, causing it to hop or rise. Because four seams are rotating at once, the ball has a greater chance of moving in the direction of the spin. A pitcher who uses an overhand delivery usually gets the ball to move straight up because his fingers are directly behind the ball. A three-quarter delivery generally gets the ball to move up and in to a right-handed batter because the ball comes off the outside of the middle finger, causing it to tail or slice. (See Photo 4.4.)

Holding the Ball with the Seams (Two-Seam Rotation)

When gripping the ball with the seams, the index and middle fingers are aligned with the two seams that are closest to each other, and the thumb is underneath the ball, on the seam. Pitchers who hold the ball with the seams generally get a sinking fastball by turning it over slightly. Turning the wrist to the outside causes the rotation of the ball to go downward and in to a right-handed batter. Every pitcher should experiment by holding the ball in various ways to see which grip gives him the most effective movement and control. (See Photo 4.5.)

The Curveball

The curveball is an effective pitch if the ball moves down or down and away from the batter. When it breaks only to the side, it remains in the hitter's contact zone for a longer period of time. It is also more difficult for the batter's eyes to adjust vertically than horizontally, making the pitch that moves down more difficult to hit. The pitcher throws a curveball with the middle and index fingers on top of the ball (see Photo 4.6), creating a pulling down action with the middle finger, which causes the ball to be released over the first and second joints of the index finger. This creates overspin and causes the ball to move

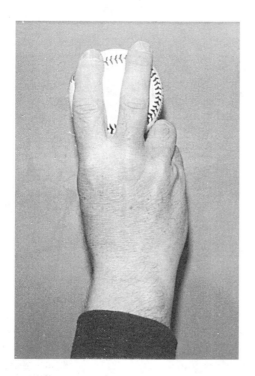

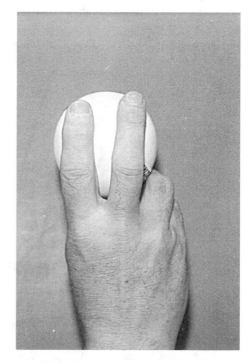

PHOTO 4.4   **PHOTO 4.5**

down. It is advisable to hold the ball with the seams, with the middle finger across the front part of the seam and the thumb resting across the bottom seam. This allows four seams to rotate as the ball comes out of the pitcher's hand.

As the pitching arm comes forward, the elbow stays high and the wrist turns inward, causing the palm of the hand to face the head. This puts the ball in a position from which it can be released with a rolling motion off the fingers. The pitcher should think "fastball" until the arm is close to the head. The elbow is now leading. The wrist turns in and snaps downward, with pressure from the index finger and thumb creating a rapid spin on the ball.

Problems that occur with a curve-ball include the following:

- Overstriding, which prevents a pulling down action with the arm.
- Dropping the elbow, which leads to short-arming the ball and causes the ball to hang.
- Thinking "curveball" too soon, which causes the pitcher to wrap his wrist and lock it.

Remember: think "fastball" until coming forward; then turn and pull.

The Slider

The slider is a late and quick-breaking pitch that results when a pitcher cuts a fastball slightly. When he makes a one-quarter inward turn of the wrist or holds the ball off center like a football (see Photo 4.7), the ball leaves the inside part of his index finger and rotates

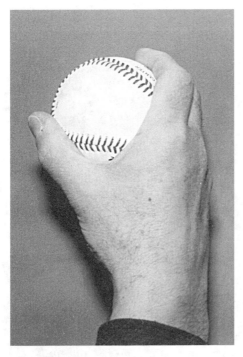

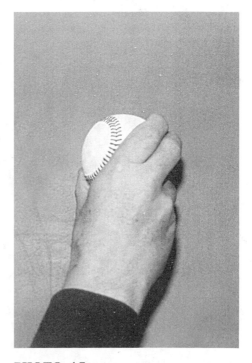

PHOTO 4.6   **PHOTO 4.7**

toward the outside part of home plate to a right-handed batter if the pitcher is right-handed. A pitcher who cannot throw an effective curveball because of his arm angle or wrist action can use a slider as a breaking pitch.

The two most common ways of teaching the slider are the off-center method of holding the ball like a football and the one-quarter inward turn of the wrist. In both cases, the middle finger applies pressure, pushing the ball off the inside part of the index finger. The slight inward turn of the wrist causes the ball to act like a fastball, breaking at the last second. It is just the opposite of a tailing fastball.

Generally a slider is effective when thrown low and away or in on the hands. It is also a good pitch when you are behind in the count and the batter zones for a fastball. Do not think of the slider as a breaking pitch. Think of it as a moving fastball.

The Change-Up

A *change-up* is a pitch that comes off the same motion and arm speed as a fastball, but with less velocity. The most effective way of throwing a change-up is to retard the wrist snap so that the ball does not have added speed. There are various ways of throwing the change-up, and a pitcher should experiment with each until he finds which is the best for him.

One method is to place the ball deep in the hand, with three fingers on top of the ball. (See Photo 4.8.) As the ball is about to be released, the pitcher lifts his fingertips up and buries the heel of his hand as though he were pulling down a window shade. By removing his fingertips from the ball and locking his wrist, he slows the ball.

Another method is to place the ball back in the palm of the hand, with three fingers on top of the ball. As the ball comes into the release area, the pitcher lets the ball roll off his

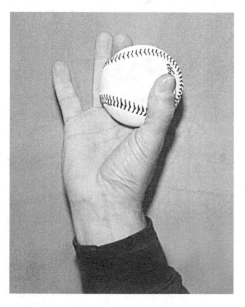

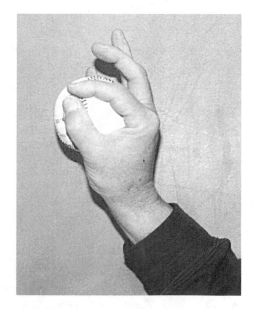

PHOTO 4.8   **PHOTO 4.9**

fingers with a slight outward turn of the wrist. This causes a slight tailing action with fast-ball spin. It is also advisable to drag the pivot foot in order to slow down the body action. This is called the *OK change*. (See Photo 4.9.)

Always try to keep the change-up low. We advise pitchers to aim to bounce the pitch on home plate, making them concentrate on a low target. The change-up allows the pitcher to upset the batter's timing and fool him many times.

LEAD-UPS TO THROWING AND PITCHING MECHANICS

- Sitting drills: A player can sit cross-legged in front of a wall, or two players can sit facing each other approximately 10 feet apart. The player with the ball places the elbow of his throwing arm in the palm of his glove and raises the elbow higher than the shoulder. (See Photo 4.10.) He grips the ball across the four seams, with fingers behind the ball and the palm of his hand facing the wall or his partner. Then he flips the ball, using only a downward wrist action. The coach and player can check the rotation of the ball (backspin) and wrist action.
- Two-knee drill: Two players face each other approximately 15–20 feet apart, kneeling on both knees. One player's throwing hand begins in the *launching position*, with fingers on top of the ball and the palm of his hand facing downward toward the ground.

PHOTO 4.10

PHOTO 4.11

(See Photo 4.11.) The player then tosses the ball to his partner while the coach watches the starting position of the hand, ensuring that the elbow stays higher than the shoulder and the fingers stay behind the ball.

- One-knee drill: Two players face each other, approximately 15–20 feet apart. Each kneels on one knee, right-handed throwers on the right and left-handed throwers on the left. One player starts with his throwing hand in his glove, in front of his body. (See Photo 4.12.) The player breaks his hand from the glove with the arm action moving downward, backward, and upward. A key phrase used to describe the arm action is *thumb to thigh, reach for the sky.*

   During the whole arm swing, the fingers stay on top of the ball, and the palm of the hand faces downward. When the hand and ball reach the launching position, the starting position of the two-knee drill, the player throws the ball to his partner and follows through, with the hand coming across the chest and finishing with the hand outside the left knee. The coach should be watching the hand break and the arm swing, ensuring that the fingers are on top of the ball, the palm is down, and the elbow is higher than the shoulder and the follow-through.

The Rotation Drill

This drill works on ball rotation and grip. It also focuses on upper body mechanics, mainly the angle of the arm and lead-arm action. The windup, pivot, and stride are eliminated,

PHOTO 4.12

enabling the pitcher to concentrate on arm movement, grip, and finger pressure, thus allowing him to see exactly how the ball is moving.

Two pitchers work together, about 30 feet apart. One pitcher does the drill while the other gets down on one knee and acts like a catcher. The pitcher throws the ball from half to three-quarter speed, and the catcher confirms the type of rotation on the ball. The catcher looks for backspin on the fastball, overspin on the curveball, or any other movement the pitcher wants.

1. The pitcher sets up with his front leg planted forward as if it were the completion of his stride. His hips are slightly open. The toes of his stride foot point directly toward the target, and his pivot foot is parallel alongside the rubber. (See Photo 4.13.)
2. His lead shoulder points toward the target in a closed position, with the glove higher than the elbow and the back of the glove facing the hitter. The pitcher's hands are away from his body, with the ball well hidden in the webbing of the glove. This is the position from which he would normally break his hands.
3. His pitching arm breaks from the glove and moves down vertically, with the wrist hanging loose and the palm of the hand facing down. This is also known as *hand break*.
4. The pitcher's arm then travels like a pendulum—going down, back, and up (thumb to thigh, reach for the sky). As this is happening, the lead shoulder remains closed.
5. As the arm reaches the launching position, the body weight remains back.
6. As the arm goes forward into the release point, it opens the lead shoulder and transfers the weight forward to the front leg.

PHOTO 4.13

7. The pitching elbow is at shoulder level or above as the pitcher's arm comes forward, while the forearm and wrist are perpendicular to the ground. The lead elbow is brought to the side, close to the hip, with the glove face out.
8. As the ball is released in what is called the *four corners,* the two shoulders and two hips are squared to the target. From this point, the pitcher can see the actual rotation of the ball and can determine how much spin was applied and the direction of the spin.
9. After the release, his arm follows through and his weight comes directly over the bent front leg. His arm ends up alongside the stride leg.

This drill is particularly valuable for coaches with no assistants. Because the coach cannot be everywhere at the same time, he can allow the pitchers to help one another.

The Pivot Drill

The key position in the delivery is the pivot. Failure to maintain balance here can impair arm-body synchronization. The loss of balance makes it difficult for the pitcher to hold his weight back, which causes his body to move forward too soon—before the arm moves. The pitcher usually ends up *rushing,* which means that his arm either drags behind his body or takes a shortcut to catch up, resulting in short-arming the ball.

Because most problems occur on the pivot, have the pitcher begin in the pivot position while working on the basic mechanics. When he gets the feel of balance and can put it all together, he can add the windup.

1. The pitcher starts in the pivot position, with his rear leg parallel to the rubber and slightly flexed. (See Photo 4.14.) He keeps his hands away from his body, about chest high at the spot in which he will break them, and brings his lead leg up in a comfortable position, with the hip pointed toward home plate. At this point, check to see whether the pitcher can hold his balance while his weight is his the rear leg.

2. The pitcher now separates his pitching hand and glove with a vertical swing of the pitching arm, which moves downward with a loose wrist. As the arm swings down, the stride leg remains up and the lead shoulder is closed and pointed toward the batter. The arm then comes up as the stride leg lands, preparing the pitcher for forward acceleration.

3. The forward movement of the arm and body comes next. The stride leg lands on the sole of the foot, rather than on the heel, with the knee bent and the toe pointed toward the plate. Although the lead leg has landed, the body weight remains back. The arm accelerates forward, opening the lead shoulder and releasing the ball with a full wrist snap. The rear foot pushes off the rubber, aiding the forward acceleration.

PHOTO 4.14

4. In the follow-through, the arm moves forward to a position alongside the front knee. The pitcher then brings his rear leg up alongside his lead leg, placing his body in a square position. The glove hand finishes alongside the hip, with the glove open.

Rotation and pivot drills can also be used by infielders and outfielders to improve their throwing mechanics.

The Pitching Delivery

The pitching delivery begins when the pitcher steps onto the rubber to receive his sign and ends when he squares off after his follow-through. The most important part of the delivery is when the pitcher gets into the pivot position, where he is balanced. This is the time to make sure he has it all together before he explodes forward.

The motion preceding the pivot is just a buildup to the power that will be applied when the pitcher goes forward and transfers his weight to the front leg.

If a pitcher has problems that cause a loss of balance or concentration in the full windup, we suggest a *no-pump windup*. This puts him into the pivot position without any wasted motion. For a pitcher who likes to build up his momentum and stretch his arms over his head, we suggest the type of delivery outlined in the next subsection. Everything here is geared to a right-handed pitcher, so all left-handers should visualize the moves from their standpoint.

Position on the Mound When Taking the Sign, with No Runners on Base

The pitcher stands up straight and relaxed, with his right foot on the right side of the rubber and the front spikes just over the front edge of the rubber. The toe of his pivot foot points slightly out, making it easier for him to rotate his body when going into the pivot. His feet are comfortably spread, with body weight equally balanced on both feet. His left foot is slightly behind and to the side of his right foot. His head, hips, and shoulders are square to home plate, with his throwing hand either in the glove about chest high or to the back and side of his right thigh. After he takes the sign, the pitcher should take a deep breath, relax, and then begin the windup.

The Windup

As the pitcher steps straight back with his left foot, his hands swing over his head with the elbows slightly out. The ball should be well hidden in the webbing of the glove so that he does not allow the batter to pick up the grip, thus tipping off the pitch. At this point, his head should remain still and face the target.

Some pitchers like to step to the side with the left foot, making it easier to rotate the body. This generally causes the head and shoulders to face toward the third-base side, which makes a pitcher's first movement toward that side rather than forward. This is called *pitching around the corner*. Because of his movement toward the third-base side first, there is a greater tendency for the pitcher to throw across his body. Actually, he should step straight back, keeping his head and shoulders square to home plate, and rotate into the pivot position. (See Photo 4.15.)

PHOTO 4.15   **PHOTO 4.16**

Body Rotation

As the hands come over the head, the ball of the right foot pivots to the right, parallel to the rubber. (See Photo 4.16.) The left knee is lifted, and the hands come down to the center of the chest. At this point, the body is rotated to the right, with the lead shoulder and hip pointing directly toward home plate. Some pitchers like to position their pivot foot half on and half off the rubber to get a better pushoff. Unless the mounds are well kept and the dirt around the rubber is hard, it is difficult for the pitcher to maintain his balance in the pivot position, especially if a deep hole has been dug in front of the rubber. (See Photo 4.17.)

The Hand Break

The pitcher's hands should break fairly high in order for his pitching arm to stretch down and swing up. The break is actually a vertical break, so the pitcher can get a swinging action and build up momentum going into the release area. An important point to remember is that the more extension the pitcher gets with the arm, the more hand speed he will get. Also keep in mind that the wrist of the pitching hand should be loose and the palm pointing down until he actually starts his forward release of the ball. This gives him a whip type of action, applying more velocity and spin to the ball.

PHOTO 4.17

The Lead Arm

It is very important that the lead shoulder remain closed until the throwing arm comes forward to open it. This helps keep the weight back and applies more power to the pitch. As the throwing hand comes through, the glove comes toward the body, palm facing the chest, with the elbow next to the left side. This puts the pitcher in better fielding position, ready for any ball hit up the middle. He should remember not to open his lead shoulder too soon, because it will open automatically as his pitching arm moves forward.

The Stride

The stride should be straight ahead, with the toe pointing directly toward home plate. This opens the hips and allows the body weight to come forward along with the arm. Be careful that the pitcher does not take too long a stride because it will be difficult for him to get his weight over a bent front leg. When the stride leg lands, it should be on the ball of the foot, with the knee slightly bent rather than on the heel, which would impair the follow-through. (See Photo 4.18.)

When the stride leg lands, the coach should be able to draw a line from the heel of the pivot foot to the heel of the stride foot. If the stride foot is landing to the left of that line, the pitcher is opening up the front side too soon. If he lands to the right of the line, he is

PHOTO 4.18

throwing across his body, not allowing his hips to open and putting additional strain on his arm.

The Follow-Through

If the lead leg is bent, the follow-through becomes automatic. If the pitcher lands on the heel of his lead leg, the leg will tend to straighten, and he will find it difficult to bend at the waist, making the follow-through incomplete. As he follows through, all of his weight is over the lead leg. The arm should snap straight across the chest and continue until it is alongside and outside the front knee. The back leg comes over parallel to the lead leg, putting him in a squared-off position. Remember: a good follow-through is important for speed, control, and proper fielding position. (See Photo 4.19.)

Here are some drills that will help your pitchers with their follow-through.

Follow-Through Drills

DRILL 4.2. Washcloth Drill

Purpose: To practice proper follow-through in pitching motion.

Area Required: Any area will do.

PHOTO 4.19

Equipment Needed: Glove and regular washcloth.

Procedure: Pitchers work in semi-slow motion through the first stages of the windup. The washcloth is held in the throwing hand. As the throwing arm reaches full extension in preparation for throwing to home plate, the pitcher must get from rear extension to front extension as quickly as possible, and the washcloth must come in contact with the ground. This is an excellent drill for teaching the fundamentals of pitching technique because the pitcher does not have to concentrate on anything but a fundamentally sound delivery. Touching the washcloth to the ground ensures that the pitcher is throwing off a soft front leg and bending the back.

DRILL 4.3.   Chair Drill

Purpose: To help the pitcher complete the follow-through with the back leg.

Area Required: Any area will do.

Equipment Needed: Folding chair, ball, and glove.

Procedure: The pitcher places his pivot foot instep on the center of the chair and points his stride foot toward the catcher. His shin and knee are not on the chair. The coach holds the pitcher's instep flat on the chair. The catcher is approximately 30 feet from the pitcher. The pitcher throws the ball at half speed to the catcher. The coach releases the pitcher's instep to allow him to bring his leg forward to complete the follow-through.

PITCHING FROM THE STRETCH POSITION

The delivery for a pitch from the stretch position must be a little faster than that from the windup position to prevent the runner from getting too big a jump. Pitchers should also learn to throw to any base from any spot while going into the stretch. Throwing from the hip with a quick dart type of throw gets the ball to the base faster than does a full arm sweep. A pitcher must work on quick leg action and fast hands to have a good pickoff move. A quick jump turn is probably the fastest way for a right-handed pitcher to get the ball to the base. A left-handed pitcher faces the runner on first base and has more of an advantage in holding him closer to the base. He can hang his leg, look at the runner, make a slight forward movement at a 45-degree angle, and still throw to the base. A right-handed pitcher must look over his left shoulder to see and check the runner. After his stride leg lifts, he must throw the ball toward home plate.

A good tip for a right-handed pitcher is to hold the ball in his bare hand when going into the stretch position. This allows him to throw to first base from any point in the stretch position. When the pitcher is ready to release the ball, he uses the same procedure he would use if he were coming out of the pivot from his regular windup. The only difference is that he may find it necessary to speed up his leg kick, hand break, and release to prevent the runner from getting too big a jump.

Taking the Sign from the Stretch Position

The pitcher places his pivot (right) foot along the front right-hand side of the rubber in a slightly flexed position. His stride leg is in front, in a closed, open, or square stance. His body is relaxed, with the ball in his pitching hand alongside his right thigh and his glove by his left thigh. His body is sideways, and he is looking toward the catcher for his sign.

After receiving the sign and while checking the runner, he brings his hands together to a position about belt high. From here, if he decides to deliver the pitch to the batter, he uses the same procedure he would use if he were pitching from the pivot position in his windup. If he decides to throw to first base, he uses a jump turn or straight body pivot.

PITCHING WITH A MAN ON THIRD BASE

With runners on third or on second and third or with bases loaded, the pitcher may use his regular windup or the stretch position. For the stretch position, he comes to a stop and looks at the runner at third base. Then he can throw to a base, throw to home plate, or step off the rubber.

If the pitcher decides to pitch from the windup position, he should follow this procedure:

1. Take the sign from the catcher.
2. Look at the runner at third base.

3. Begin the windup and throw to home plate. If the runner breaks toward home plate before the pitcher starts his windup, the pitcher should step off the rubber and make the play. After the pitcher steps off the rubber, he is considered an infielder, and the batter cannot swing at the ball being thrown toward home plate.

USING FILMS TO REVIEW FUNDAMENTALS AND MECHANICS

Watching films of their actions can be very helpful to pitchers. As they review the films, have them consider the following:

1. Watch the feet first.

   - Do you overstride or understride? If you land on your heel, you are overstriding.
   - Do you throw across your body or open up too soon?
   - After the ball is delivered, are you in proper fielding position?
   - When pitching from the stretch, are you lifting your leg high and cradling your body?
   - Also from the stretch, do you swing your leg around to gain more motion? This causes you to unload too slowly.

2. Watch your arm and body.

   - Do you follow through and bend your back after delivering the ball? Never become a straight-up pitcher.
   - Is your arm moving forward quickly, or is it a lazy arm?
   - Do you throw all of your pitches from the same position?
   - Can you or the coach call your pitches from the film?
   - From the stretch, does your arm have actions as fast as those of your legs and body? This is very important.

3. Watch your head.

   - Do you keep your eyes set on the target and your head still?
   - From the stretch, do you vary your looks to the bases?
   - Do you vary your head movements to bases?

        Good fastball pitchers all have quick forward-moving arms. If a pitcher's arm is lazy, he can see it by watching films. Like hitters, pitchers can get into slumps. By using films, a pitcher can compare his good outings with his bad. This way he can notice and correct his faults in a short time. Pitchers and coaches should watch game films and practice films.

WARM-UP PROCEDURES

TIPS FOR THE STARTER

- Throw from a pitcher's mound if one is available.
- Throw at the same angle and direction as you would from the mound on the game field.
- Vary the length of warm-up, depending on temperature and wind conditions, type of musculature, and past experience.
- Always do some jogging, stretching, and loosening-up exercises before starting to throw.
- Spend at least half of the warm-up time throwing at medium to three-quarter speed, concentrating on control.
- Use all pitches during the warm-up: fastball, curve, change-up, and so on.
- Make sure that some throwing is done from the set position.
- It is better to warm up too much rather than too little. The dangerous parts of the game for the pitcher are innings one, two, eight, and nine. (This parallels the piloting of a plane: the two most dangerous parts of the flight are the takeoff and landing.)
- Always warm up by throwing to spots inside, outside, high, and low in the strike zone.
- Throw the last fifteen pitches of the warm-up in the bull pen at game velocity.
- Keep the first few warm-up pitches on the game mound down at medium speed until the footing for the stride is established.

TIPS FOR THE RELIEVER

- Pay attention, know the score, and know the number of outs and the game situation.
- Hurry, don't hesitate when told to warm up.
- If needed in a hurry, play catch quickly at a short distance, and continue the regular routine.
- Be ready even if you are never called on to pitch during a game. Keep tossing at medium speed and concentrating on control until directed otherwise.
- Run to the mound when you are called into the game, become familiar with the mound, and take your warm-ups from the stretch or windup position, depending on the game situation.
- Be ready with your best pitch.

Reminder for coaches: Have someone in the bull pen keep the pitcher informed about what is happening in the game. The pitcher and catcher should not stop to watch the game between pitches.

5

DRILLS FOR A COHESIVE UNIT: PITCHERS, CATCHERS, AND INFIELDERS

PITCHING DRILLS

When you have taught your players the basic pitching mechanics, you will be ready to start building a pitching program geared to your own team's strengths and needs. This chapter deals with drills that will enable your team to become a fine defensive unit and handle any situation that arises during a game. These drills will help make your pitchers and infield a finely tuned, cohesive unit.

TEN FUNDAMENTAL FIELDING SITUATIONS

A pitcher must be skilled in delivering the ball to home plate and must be in control of the strike zone with all of his pitches, and he also must be able to field his position when the ball is hit to him. Not only must he field the ball, but he must also know what to do with it.

Many pitchers, when they get into trouble and have men on base, concentrate so much on the hitter that they forget what to do when the ball is hit *to* them. The drills in this chapter will help the pitcher and infielders communicate with each other. Through constant repetition of the drills, their reactions to situations will become automatic.

1. Fielding bunts and topped rollers: Use skip-step when possible.
   • No runners on base: throw to first base.
   • Runner on first base: force at second base, if possible.
   • Runners on first and second bases: force at third base.
   • Runner on second base only: tag play at third base.

2. The comeback ball: Use the skip-step.
   - No runners on base: wait for first baseman to get to the base, and then throw hard.
   - Runner on first base: throw to second baseman or shortstop covering the base.
   - Runners on first and second bases: use 1-6-3 or 1-4-3 double play.
   - Bases loaded: use 1-2-3 double play, making sure of out at home plate.
3. Backing up bases: Get off the mound quickly.
   - Stand 35–40 feet behind the base, if possible. Make sure to block the ball. Keep it in front of you.
   - Go the short way off the mound.
   - If in doubt, go halfway between bases and see how the play develops.
   - With no one on base and the batter hitting a single, keep an eye on the ball in case of a deflected throw. This is called *having a nose for the ball.*
4. Covering first base: Break off the mound hard on all balls hit to your left. Stay on the inside part of the foul line, and touch the inside corner of the base with your right foot.
5. Covering second base: When the shortstop and second baseman both go after a short fly ball in center field, break hard to second base.
6. Covering third base: When there is a fly ball down the left-field line and both the third baseman and shortstop go for it, break hard for third base.
7. Covering home plate: For all wild pitches and passed balls with runners on base, if the catcher cannot locate the ball, run in, pointing at the ball, and tell him in a loud voice where it is. This makes use of both visual and verbal signs. Also cover when the catcher goes for a foul fly with runners on base.
8. Covering comeback plays: Charge a runner who is hung up on a comeback ball, run him back toward the base he came from, and give the ball up to an infielder as soon as possible, continuing into a backup position.
9. Runner on first base breaks prematurely while the pitcher is in the set position: Step back off the pitching rubber with the pivot foot. Do not break your hands first.
10. Runners on first and third: When the runner on first breaks prematurely, step back off the pitching rubber, turn by way of third base to check and hold the runner, and then throw to the second baseman in a *cheating* position.

PICKOFFS AT SECOND BASE

Daylight

1. Infielders must give up territory at shortstop and second base at the start of the play.
2. The shortstop moves in behind the runner while the pitcher is in the stretch position.
3. The shortstop backs off slowly toward center field. When the pitcher can see daylight between the runner and the shortstop, he turns and throws to second base.
4. If the shortstop backs away from the runner toward his regular position, the pitcher throws to home plate.
5. If the pitcher does not throw to second base, he should be sure to give the shortstop enough time to get back to his position or step back off the rubber.

In and Out

1. A signal should be arranged between the pitcher, shortstop, and second baseman to initiate the play.
2. The shortstop gives the signal before the pitcher goes into the stretch position.
3. The shortstop moves in behind the runner as in the daylight play and chases the runner back to second base.
4. As the shortstop backs off toward his normal position, the second baseman watches to see when the runner begins to move toward third base. When he begins to move, the second baseman breaks for the base.
5. As the pitcher sees the second baseman break, he turns and throws to second base.
6. Timing is very important in this play and must be worked on in practice.

Blind Pickoff

This play is used when the bases are loaded, or with runners on second and third bases, and the pitcher is in the windup position.

1. The runner on second base feels secure because he has a runner in front of him and the pitcher is in the windup position with his back to him. He usually wanders off the base farther than usual.
2. The catcher gives a prearranged sign to the shortstop and the pitcher before the pitcher steps on the rubber.
3. When the pitcher is on the rubber, looking for the sign, the shortstop breaks directly for second base. When the catcher sees the shortstop break for second base, he gives a sign to the pitcher to turn and throw to second base. This sign could be dropping his glove from the target position. The pitcher throws the ball directly over second base.

   Timing is essential and must be practiced constantly because of the difficulty of the throw to be made by the pitcher.

PRECISION DRILLS FOR PITCHERS

Fielding Bunts and Topped Rollers

In the first half of the drill with no runner on, the pitcher throws with a full windup. He changes to the stretch for the last half of the drill, when a runner is on first base. The first baseman plays the deep position. The pitcher throws with the full windup and holds the runner on base when the stretch position is used. The second baseman plays his normal position until the stretch position is used. Then he shortens up and shades slightly toward second base. The third baseman plays his normal position until the stretch position is used. Then he plays one or two steps in on the grass. The catcher is in his regular receiving stance behind home plate.

With No Runners on Base

The pitcher delivers, using a full windup. After receiving the pitch, the catcher or coach tosses a bunt or simulated roller in front of home plate. Easy pitches should be tossed to start; when the pitcher is warmed up, more difficult ones can be rolled down the foul lines. The pitcher must hustle off the mound and get to the ball as quickly as possible with his body under control, field the ball in front of him with two hands, take an aggressive step toward first base, and throw hard to the first baseman, aiming at his face. The second baseman backs up the first baseman, the shortstop covers second base, the third baseman covers third base, and the catcher, calling the play loud and clear, points to where the ball is to be thrown and then covers home plate. (See Figure 5.1.)

With a Runner on First Base

The pitcher delivers, using the stretch position. The catcher or coach tosses a simulated bunt. The pitcher goes through the same procedure, throwing to either the first or second baseman, whoever is covering. The pitcher concentrates on keeping his throws to the inside of the diamond to avoid hitting the runner. Throwing over the runner makes it difficult for the first or second baseman to see the throw.

The first baseman charges if he has a play or backs up to take the throw if he does not. The second baseman waits until the bunt is down and then breaks to cover first base. The

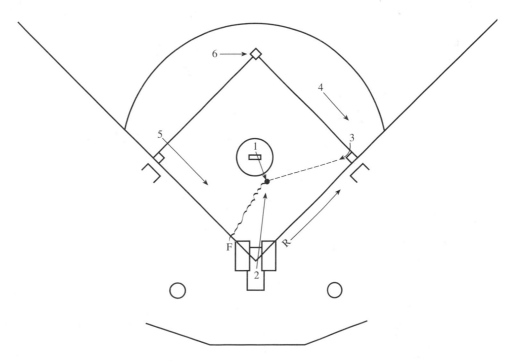

FIGURE 5.1

second baseman's first step should be toward home plate and then toward first base. This protects against the fake bunt/slash and the hit and run. If the first baseman has backed up to take the throw, the second baseman backs up the first baseman. The shortstop waits until the bunt is down and then proceeds to cover second base. The third baseman charges, with his body under control and his hands ready as the pitcher delivers the ball. He must be aware of the fake bunt/slash. If the pitcher fields the ball, the third baseman retreats and covers third base. The catcher repeats the previous routine and calls the play "first" or "second" in this case. If the third baseman fields the ball, the catcher continues on to cover third base.

The second or first baseman, whoever covers, must be facing the throw and giving a good inside target with his hands. He should have his left foot on the base and be ready to receive the throw. Although this drill is designed primarily for pitchers, the catcher or coach may toss a bunt to the first baseman, third baseman, or catcher to simulate those game situations. (See Figure 5.2.)

With Runners on First and Second Bases

The pitcher throws from the stretch position. The catcher is in his normal receiving position behind the plate. The first baseman plays from two to three steps in on the grass and charges with his body under control as the pitcher delivers. He is responsible for any bunt from the first-base line to the pitcher's mound. The second baseman shortens up and shades toward first base. When the bunt is down, he covers first base. The shortstop shortens up slightly, perhaps three or four steps behind and just off the right shoulder of the runner. He

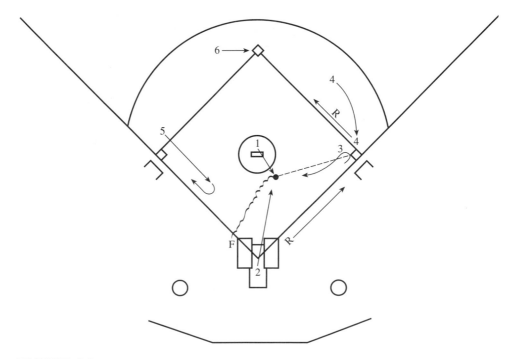

FIGURE 5.2

wants the runner to shorten his lead. When the bunt is down, he covers second base. The third baseman plays one step in on the grass and advances one more step as the pitcher delivers. He then holds to see how the play develops.

The pitcher delivers the ball to home plate and after his follow-through breaks to a spot on the third-base line about one-third of the way from home plate to third base, approximately 30 feet. He has his body under control and is responsible for all bunts on the third-base line. He does not wait until the ball is bunted, but breaks immediately to the spot described after delivering the pitch. The first baseman is responsible for any balls bunted behind the charging pitcher. The pitcher gets to the bunt as quickly as possible, fields the ball with both hands out in front, and whirls to his glove-hand side. With a strong forearm flip he throws to the third baseman, who, seeing that the pitcher will field the ball, has retreated to third base to take the throw. If possible, the third baseman stretches out like a first baseman to complete the play.

In making his throw after fielding the bunt, the pitcher must concentrate on whirling and throwing in one motion to avoid losing time. If he straightens up and draws his arm way back *(winds up),* he will lose precious time to the runner, who is in full stride. He should aim his quick, short, forearm flip at the third baseman's face, where it will be easy to handle on a stretch.

The third baseman fields any sharply bunted ball that gets by the pitcher and fires to second or first, as directed by the catcher, who once again calls the play. The first baseman fields all bunts in his area and with a skip-step fires to third, if that is the call, or to first. He must be aggressive and expect to make the play on the lead runner at third base. The catcher breaks out to field any short bunt immediately in front of plate and fires to third base if there is a play there. If not fielding the bunt, he calls the play for the pitcher, third baseman, and first baseman. The catcher is the only player on the field who has all of the runners in front of him. Thus he can see the play develop and make the right call.

We have purposely delayed outlining the most important part of this drill and have taken it out of its natural sequence to emphisize that if this technique is not mastered, your players will have a very difficult time getting the lead runner. Remember that the shortstop plays just off the right shoulder of the runner at second base and fairly deep, perhaps four steps back and trying to shorten his lead. The pitcher comes to his set or stretch position and looks back at second base. Simultaneously, the shortstop breaks behind the runner toward second base. The runner, losing sight of the shortstop over his right shoulder and possibly hearing a warning from his third base coach, is forced to break back to second base. Even with a smaller lead, he shifts his body weight from his right to his left foot and leans toward second base. When the pitcher sees this happen, he immediately delivers to home plate.

Thus we have the ball bunted when the lead runner is moving or, at the very least, leaning in the wrong direction. If all the fielders do their jobs properly, you have a good chance of cutting down the lead runner and breaking up a big inning. (See Figure 5.3.)

With a Runner on Second Base Only and a Bunt in Order
If there is a runner on second base only, the techniques are exactly the same except for the duties carried out by the third baseman. Before the play begins, remind the players that in case of a bunt, the third baseman retreats to third base, straddles the base, receives the throw, and tags the sliding runner.

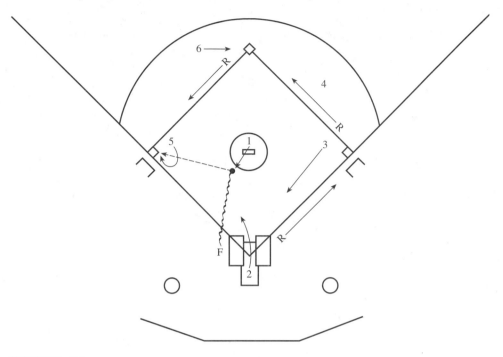

FIGURE 5.3

The catcher, in calling the play, realizes that the pitcher has less time before making the throw to third base. The pitcher should aim knee high to help make the tag easier and faster. If the third baseman judges that the pitcher will not be able to field the bunt, he should charge, field the bunt, and throw the runner out at first base. Remember: it is extremely important that in these situations (runner on first base, runners on first and second bases, and runner on second base only), we record an out, even if it is only at first base. (See Figure 5.4.)

Comeback Ball

With runners on first base or first and second bases, the infield is set at double-play depth. The pitcher works from the stretch position. He checks the position of the shortstop as he would during the game because they will work together in the event of a comeback ball. The shortstop gives the sign to the pitcher, revealing whether he or the second baseman will cover the base on a comebacker.

Using the stretch position, the pitcher delivers to home plate. The coach, standing close to home plate with a fungo bat and extra ball, hits a comebacker to the pitcher. The pitcher fields the ball out in front with both hands, if possible, whirls to his glove-hand side, and takes an aggressive skip-step toward second base. The pitcher's job is to lead the shortstop, who is breaking toward second base. The shortstop catches the ball, touches second base, and throws to first base to complete the double play. If the shortstop is slow in getting into motion or has a long way to go, the pitcher may take an extra skip-step to time the

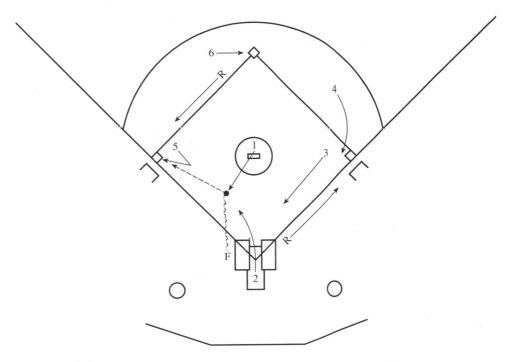

FIGURE 5.4

play and to keep himself in motion toward his target, thus cutting down on the possibility of a wild throw or injury.

On the play, the second baseman backs up the shortstop at second base, the first baseman covers first base, the third baseman covers third base, and the catcher covers home plate. With a runner on first base only, there is only one change. The first baseman holds the runner on, rather than playing behind him in double-play depth.

You will find it profitable to spend a few minutes on the same play with the second baseman as the pivot man. If a strong right-handed pull hitter should be at the plate, the shortstop would be fairly deep and toward the third-base hole; the second baseman would be only a few steps from second base. In this case, as the pitcher whirls to his glove-hand side and takes the skip-step, the second baseman has already reached the base. The pitcher should throw the ball face high, just over the first-base side of second base. The catcher, as always, points and calls the play. (See Figure 5.5.)

With the Bases Loaded
With bases loaded and fewer than two outs, the catcher reminds the pitcher to come home with the comebacker. The pitcher practices his short windup (set position) with a runner on third base and delivers to home plate. The catcher is in his normal receiving position behind home plate.

The shortstop and second baseman are at double-play depth. The first and third basemen play opposite their respective bases and judge the distance from the foul line accord-

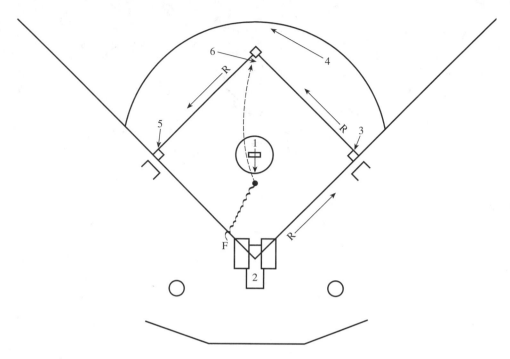

FIGURE 5.5

ing to the hitter. The second baseman and shortstop look for a double play in the middle or a force at home plate, depending on the speed of the ground ball. The third baseman and first baseman look for a force at home plate and possibly a double play at first base on the hitter, on all ground balls that they must charge, whether hit directly at them, to the foul-line side, or at half speed. On hard ground balls to the second-base side, they try for the double play via second base and back to first base.

The coach hits a comebacker to the pitcher, who fields the ball out in front with both hands. He then takes a skip-step toward home plate and makes a quick dart throw to the catcher at home plate. The pitcher should have in mind accuracy, not power. If he throws the ball too hard, he will handcuff the catcher and reduce the possibility of a double play.

When the ball is hit to the pitcher, the catcher comes up and plants his right foot on home plate, with his hands high and ready for the throw. If it is accurate, he catches the ball while moving out with a skip-step into the diamond and up toward first base. He should do this aggressively, to clear himself from the runner attempting to score from third base and to take himself well inside the runner going to first base. Now he has an easy throw to the first baseman, who should be giving him a good inside target.

The third baseman covers third base, the second baseman and shortstop cover second base and back up second base, and the first baseman covers first base. Once in a while, make the catchers go through these drills with full catcher's equipment so that they get used to making the plays under game conditions. (See Figure 5.6.)

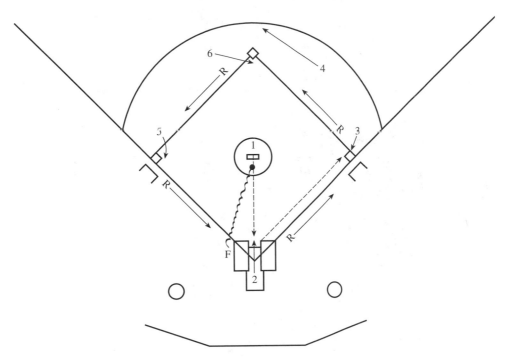

FIGURE 5.6

Pitcher Covering First Base

Whenever a left-handed hitter comes to home plate, or a right-handed hitter who is a late swinger is at bat, the catcher and first baseman remind the pitcher to get off the mound fast and cover first base in the event of a ground ball to the right side of the infield.

With No Runners on Base

The pitcher takes his full windup, the catcher is in his normal receiving position behind home plate, and the infield is playing deep. The coach, once again, is next to home plate with a fungo bat and an extra ball.

When the pitcher delivers the ball to the catcher, the coach hits a ground ball to the first baseman. When the ball is hit, but not before, the pitcher breaks hard, with his body under control, to a spot approximately 20 feet from the first-base line. He turns and runs parallel with the foul line toward first base, with both of his hands up as a target for the first baseman. The pitcher must be sure to run up the inside of the first-base line to avoid interference with the runner, who must run outside the foul line for the last 45 feet.

The first baseman, who has fielded the ball, must now feed the moving pitcher quickly and accurately. For balls hit to him or to the foul-line side, he takes several steps toward first base and lobs a soft underhand toss to the pitcher coming up the inside of the foul line. He takes the ball out of his glove and shows it to the pitcher as he prepares to make his

PHOTO 5.1

underhand toss. He aims his toss chest high and to the inside of the base. In addition, he tries to get the ball to the pitcher a few steps before he reaches the base so that he can glance down and make sure that he touches the base. The pitcher receives the throw, touches the inside corner of the base, and bounces off aggressively into the infield. (See Photo 5.1.) This action avoids contact and chance of injury to himself or the base runner.

When the pitcher is coming off the base into the infield, make him keep his hands letter high, whirl to his glove side, face the infield, and cock his arm ready to throw. This part of the drill prepares the pitcher to make the next play when another runner may be trying to advance. You must insist on second effort and mental alertness.

On a ball hit deep to the second-base side of the first baseman, or on a ball that is fumbled by the first baseman, the pitcher should stop at the base if he has time and stretch like a first baseman to complete the play. (See Figure 5.7.)

With a Runner on First Base
The pitcher uses his stretch position, and the catcher is in his normal receiving position behind home plate. The infield is set at double-play depth, and the first baseman holds the runner on the base. When the pitcher delivers the ball to the catcher, the coach hits a ground ball wide to the second-base side of first base. The first baseman, who has broken off the

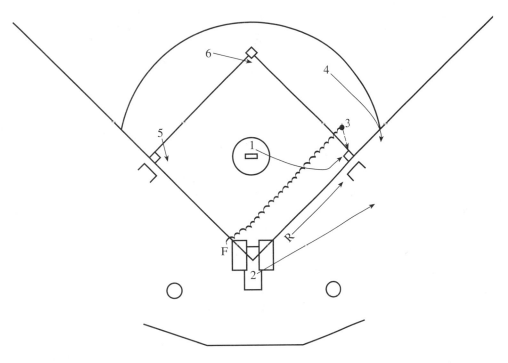

FIGURE 5.7

base on the pitch, continues to his right and fields the ball. He throws to the shortstop, who has rounded into second base on the inside corner. Because the first baseman was holding the runner on base, he fields the ball on the grass. This throw to the inside avoids any trouble with the runner who is going from first to second base.

The pitcher breaks over as quickly as possible to cover first base. The first baseman, going well to his right, cannot come back to cover first base. The pitcher straddles first base, facing second base this time, and receives the return throw from the shortstop. He tries to stretch out as a first baseman would to complete the play.

Sometimes pitchers start to anticipate and break toward first base before the coach hits the ball. A quick cure is a bunt down the third-base line rather than a ground ball to the right side. The pitcher looks bad breaking to first base when he should be fielding a bunt. The lesson stays with him, and he usually gets some good-natured ribbing from his teammates. (See Figure 5.8.)

More Pitching Drills

Following are more pitchers' fielding practice drills used by various coaches from around the country.

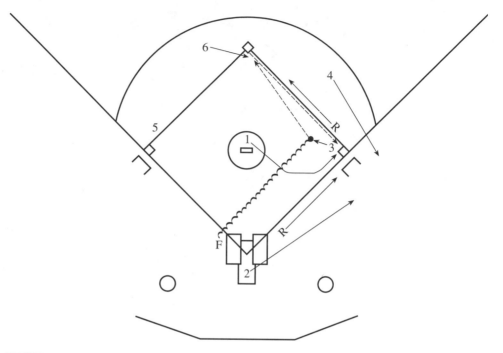

FIGURE 5.8

DRILL 5.1. Pitchers' Fielding Practice

Purpose: To cover most of the fielding plays that a pitcher will experience in a game.

Area Required: An infield.

Equipment Needed: A fungo bat and a baseball for each pitcher.

Procedure: Each pitcher has a ball and makes a line behind the mound. All infielders, including the catchers are at their positions. The first pitcher winds up and throws the ball to the catcher. Then the coach hits a fungo to begin each drill. Each pitcher goes through the drill and then moves to the next step.

1. On a ground ball to first base, the pitcher covers first base.
2. With a simulated runner at second base, a ground ball is hit to first base. The pitcher covers first base and after tagging the base looks toward the runner at third base to prevent him from advancing to home plate.
3. On ground balls back to the pitcher,
    a. Check the runner at second base, then throw to first base.
    b. Check the runner at third base, then throw to first base.
    c. With a simulated runner at first base, turn double play using second baseman.
    d. With a simulated runner at first base, turn double play using shortstop.

4. With a simulated runner at first base, roll a bunt out and let the pitcher decide to throw to first base or second base, depending on the speed of the ball.
5. With a simulated runner at second base, roll a bunt out and let the pitcher decide to throw to third base or first base, depending on the speed of the ball.
6. Put a runner at third base, and make the pitcher go from the windup. The pitcher checks the runner before he starts his windup. If the runner does not leave early, the pitcher delivers a breaking ball to the plate. If the runner leaves early, he throws a pitch out.
7. Simulating that bases are loaded, hit a ground ball back to the mound. The pitcher fields the ball and throws to the catcher for the force out. The catcher then delivers the ball to first base.
8. The pitcher delivers the ball to the plate. The coach rolls a ball behind the catcher, as though it were a short, passed ball. The pitcher covers home plate while the catcher slides and throws the ball to the pitcher.

DRILL 5.2.   Baylock 3–1 Drill

Purpose: To give pitchers practice with three basic defensive plays with infielders. They can perform the drill before and during the season.

Area Required: Baseball field or gym.

Procedure: The coach at home plate initiates the start of the drill with a vocal signal—now—or by clicking two bats together. (See Figure 5.9.)

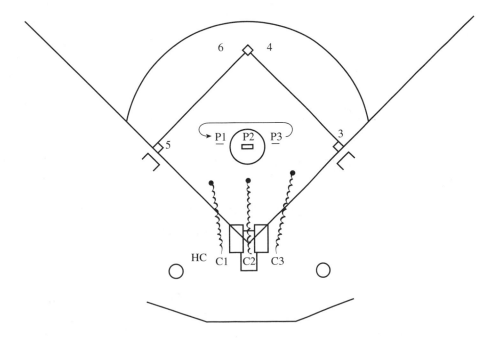

FIGURE 5.9

Pitchers: Shoulder to shoulder on the mound in follow-through position.

Catchers: Shoulder to shoulder at home plate.

Initiate Drill: On coach's signal, catchers roll balls.

> C1 rolls a bunt toward third base; P1 fields the bunt and throws to third base.
> C2 rolls a comebacker to the mound; P2 fields the ball and throws to second base for a double play.
> C3 rolls the ball to the right side of the infield; P3 makes a 3–1 or 1–3 play.

Phase I: Do drill several times, *no ball.*
Phase II: Do drill many times, *use a ball.*
Phase III: Do drill with one pitcher on the mound. He must react no matter where the ball is rolled.

DRILL 5.3.   Three-Pitcher Drill

Purpose: To give fielding practice to pitchers, catchers, and infielders.

Area Required: Baseball field, gym floor, or parking lot.

Equipment Needed: Balls, bases, three home plates, and two fungo bats.

Procedure: Pitchers are on the mound in three lines. Catchers are behind home plate in three lines. Infielders are at their positions.

(Figure 5.10 illustrates the drill and who is working in each group. The throws are made to the bases that are closest to the fielding pitcher. This is to prevent pitchers throwing across the line of other pitchers' throws.)

Group 1:   Works on covering first base, comebackers throwing to first base, fielding bunts and throwing to first base, catcher fielding bunts and throwing to first base, and ground balls to second base with the pitcher covering first base.

Group 2:   Works on comebackers throwing to second base, fielding bunts and throwing to second base, pitchers covering home plate on passed ball, and pitchers fielding bunts and underhand tosses to catcher for force play.

Group 3:   The pitcher fields bunts and throws to third base, the third baseman fields slow rollers and throws to home plate for force play. (See Figure 5.10.)

DRILL 5.4.   Pitchers' Fielding Practice—Four-Man Drill

Purpose: To give pitchers practice in all fielding situations.

Area Required: Infield or gym.

Equipment Needed: Balls, bases, and four home plates.

Procedure: Get twelve pitchers working on defensive situations as follows: Place four pitchers on the mound (P1, P2, P3, P4). P1 fields a slow roller and throws to third base. P2 covers home plate and receives the throw from C1 at the backstop. P3 fields a comebacker and throws to second base. P4 covers first base. You can put either

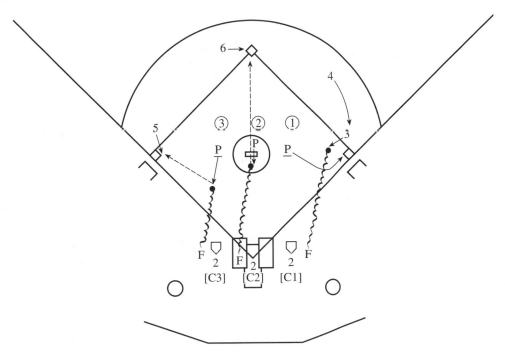

FIGURE 5.10

infielders or pitchers at the bases. Pitchers at the bases get an opportunity to handle throws and make tags, which they do not practice very often. P11 rolls the ball for P1. P33 rolls a comebacker to P3. P44 rolls the ball for P4 to cover first base. (See Figure 5.11.)

DRILL 5.5. Olson: 3–1 Drill

Purpose: To incorporate defensive drills for pitchers.

Area Required: Infield or gym.

Equipment Needed: Bases and home plate.

Procedure: All pitchers are on the mound. Catchers are behind home plate. Infielders are at their positions.

Phase I: The pitcher delivers the ball to the catcher, the coach hits a fungo ground ball to first base, and the pitcher covers.

Phase II: A second pitcher delivers the ball to the catcher, and the coach hits a fungo back up the middle or to the left or right of the pitcher. The pitcher fields the ball and throws to second base. The proper infielder covers and delivers the ball to first base to complete the double play.

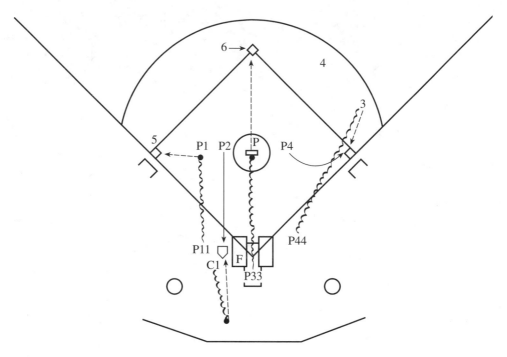

FIGURE 5.11

Phase III: A third pitcher delivers the ball to the catcher. A coach bunts the ball down the third-base line. The pitcher or third baseman must field the ball and make the play called by the catcher. As a coach, you can add many more variations to this drill to improve the pitchers' fielding ability.

DRILL 5.6.   Pitchers' Fielding Seven-in-One Drill

Purpose: To improve defensive skills of pitchers and infielders.

Area Required: Infield or gym.

Equipment Needed: Bases, home plate, fungo bat, and balls.

Procedure: Each pitcher has a ball. As the play unfolds, the next pitcher sprints to the mound. Pitchers are lined up outside the third-base foul line.

Sequence: 1. 3-1 ground ball (1B deep and off line)
                2. 3-6-1/3 DP (1B holding runner on)
                3. 1-4-3 DP (Comebacker)
                4. 1-6-3 DP (Comebacker)
                5. 2-6-4 (Catcher throws down on SB attempt)
                6. 5-4-3 DP
                7. 5-3/1-3 (Slow roller/bunt)
                Continue the sequence.

DRILL 5.7.   Pitchers' Awareness Drill

Purpose: To give the pitcher an awareness of where he is on the field when the ball is bunted to him and to improve physical and mental reaction. Pitchers must be able to think and react at the same time.

Area Required: Any flat area approximately 60 feet square, indoors or outdoors.

Equipment Needed: Four bases and a ball.

Procedure: Place four pitchers in a square approximately 60 feet apart. Each of the four pitchers represents a base. Place one pitcher in the center of the square with a ball. (See Figure 5.12.)

The pitcher in the center (P1) throws the ball to P2. P2 now becomes the catcher. P3 becomes 1B, P4 becomes 2B, and P5 becomes 3B. The catcher (P2) receives the ball, rolls it toward the pitcher (P1), and yells out a base. Let's say that you use 1, 2, 3, and 4 as commands for first, second, third, and home. The catcher (P2) yells "One." The pitcher (P1) fields the ball and throws to the first baseman (P3).

As the first baseman (P3) receives the ball, he becomes the catcher. P4 becomes 1B, P5 becomes 2B, and P2 becomes 3B. When the pitcher (P1) is set back in the middle of the square, the catcher (P3) makes another call and rolls the ball. The pitcher fields the ball and makes the play accordingly.

We find this drill extremely effective because the pitcher must react to the call by the catcher, must align his feet properly to throw to the base called, and must remember that the positions of the bases change each time he throws the ball. The players

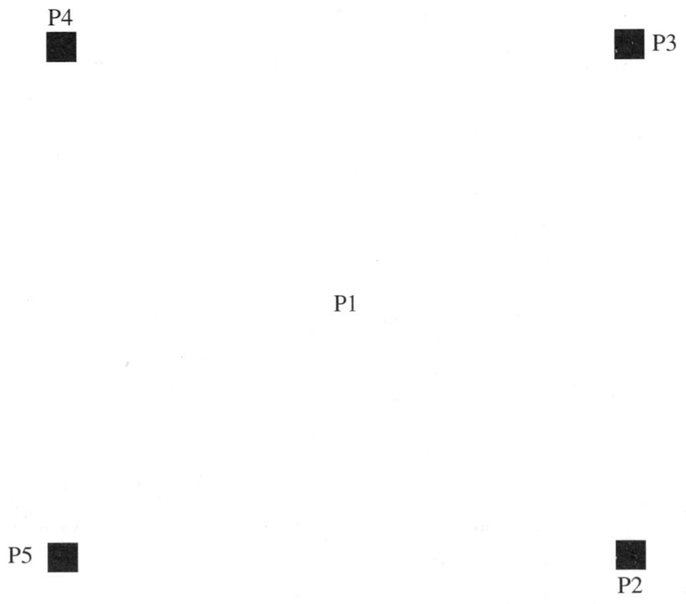

FIGURE 5.12

may be confused at first because what was home for the pitcher on the first throw may become first, second, or third on the second throw. It is important that the person making the call yell out the command clearly before rolling the ball. This gives the pitcher the opportunity to approach the ball at the proper angle to make his throw. This is a great conditioning drill for pitchers.

DRILL 5.8.   Quick Reaction Drill

Purpose: To teach pitchers quick reactions on a ball hit through the middle. Also used for infielders.

Area Required: A flat area by a high fence or the backstop.

Equipment Needed: Fungo bat and balls.

Procedure: Have the pitcher stand 8–10 feet in front of the fence or backstop. The coach stands 30–40 feet away from the pitcher. He starts throwing balls into the dirt directly in front of the pitcher and lets him react to them. Then he throws balls to the pitcher's right and left. The pitcher fields the balls with his glove hand only. He keeps his pitching hand away from the ball. The coach can then move back and use the fungo to hit the ground balls.

DRILL 5.9.   Floating Strike Zone

Purpose: To teach a pitcher who is struggling with control to throw strikes.

Area Required: 60 feet, 6 inches.

Equipment Needed: Home plate.

Procedure: The pitcher loosens up with the catcher. The catcher stands behind home plate, 3 feet to the left of the plate. The pitcher throws three pitches to the catcher. The catcher moves to a position 3 feet to the right of home plate, and the pitcher throws three pitches to him in this position. Then the catcher moves directly behind home plate, and the pitcher throws three pitches to him in this position.

The pitcher concentrates on the catcher more because he is outside the strike zone, and he steps directly toward the catcher with his stride leg when the target is outside the strike zone. Have pitchers work on all of their pitches while the catcher is moving right, left, and down the middle.

DRILL 5.10.   Curveball Drill for Pitchers

Purpose: To teach the pitcher the proper grip and rotation on the curveball.

Area Required: A flat area approximately 30 feet long.

Equipment Needed: A baseball with a black line drawn in the middle, in the direction in which the seams run.

Procedure: Two pitchers stand about 30 feet apart and throw the ball to one another. Each grips the ball with the middle finger and thumb running along the seams.

One pitcher throws the ball while the other looks for the proper rotation and break. The four seams and the black line should have overspin. If the spin is to the side, the receiver reminds the pitcher to get his fingers on top of the ball rather than to the side. The marked ball can also be used in the rotation drill described previously.

DRILL 5.11. String Target Strike Zone

Purpose: To help the pitcher develop control and focus on a visual strike zone.

Area Required: 60 feet, 6 inches.

Equipment Needed: Poles and string to set up strike zone.

Procedure: Place two poles 4 to 5 feet apart on either side of home plate so that a string fastened to each pole will cross above the direct center of home plate. Tie three strings across home plate, one at the top of the strike zone (letters), one waist high, and one at the bottom of the strike zone (knees). At the center of the strings, directly over the center of the plate, tie a vertical string from the top horizontal string to the bottom one. Then tie two other vertical strings so that one comes exactly to the edge of one side of home plate and the other is at the opposite edge, making the distance between these outside strings the width of home plate.

This gives a window type target that is divided into four quadrants. The quadrants represent a place for each pitch: high inside, low inside, high outside, and low outside, giving the pitcher a visual picture of the strike zone. The pitcher throws at the various quadrants, wherever the catcher has placed his glove as a target. The catcher should be in full catcher's equipment. The pitcher throws all of his pitches to sharpen his control.

DRILL 5.12. Pitchers Backup Drill

Purpose: To teach the pitcher position and depth of backup position.

Area Required: Infield and foul ball area.

Equipment Needed: Fungo bat and baseballs.

Procedure: All pitchers are on the mound. The coach hits the fungos from the infield dirt area. The first pitcher on the mound sprints to the warning track or fence behind third base. The coach hits a fungo as if the throw were coming from center field or right field. The pitcher must block the ball from going into the dugout or hitting the fence. He must keep the ball in front of him. The same procedure can be used for backing up home plate.

DRILL 5.13. Pitcher Reverse Drill

Purpose: To teach pitchers to react to a ball hit to 1B/RF.

Area Required: Infield.

Equipment Needed: Fungo bat and baseballs.

Procedure: The pitcher delivers the ball to home plate. The fungo hitter hits a ground ball wide of first base. The pitcher breaks to cover first base. If the first baseman fields the ball, the pitcher covers first base. If the ball gets past the first baseman and goes into right field, the pitcher reverses his direction and sprints to back up third base. You can also put a runner on first base, have the second baseman try for the ball, too, and have the right fielder make the throw to third base to try to retire the runner.

DRILL 5.14.   Dummy Batter Target

Purpose: To simulate a hitter in the batter's box while the pitcher is throwing.

Area Required: Pitcher's mound or warm-up area.

Equipment Needed: Broomstick or pole and a piece of Styrofoam. Make a dummy from the broomstick or a pole. Stick the pole in the ground in the batter's box. Put a head on the pole: a round piece of Styrofoam. Paint a face on it, put a hat on it, be creative.

Procedure: The pitcher throws to a catcher with the dummy in either batter's box. The pitcher can work on his control, especially the up-and-in pitch, without fear of hurting one of his teammates. The dummy won't complain if it is hit. The pitcher can work on all of his pitches with the feeling that a hitter is in the batter's box at all times.

6

CATCHING: QUALITIES THAT GO BEYOND THE PHYSICAL

THE QUALITIES TO LOOK FOR IN A CATCHER

1. Leadership potential: Every team needs a leader on the field—a man who takes charge and quarterbacks the team. The catcher directs the team on the field. He takes charge, sees everything in front of him, directs, keeps his teammates on their toes, and calls the game for his pitcher.
2. Physical strength: The catcher should be rugged and durable. He must be ready for contact, willing to get his uniform dirty, and able to use his body to block pitches in the dirt.
3. Quickness and agility: Games are won and lost because of the catcher's failure to shift his weight quickly in blocking or catching a poorly thrown ball. The catcher must be agile in shifting for pitches, fielding bunts, and catching pop-ups.
4. Good throwing arm: The catcher must have a strong arm and a quick release. A quick release can help to compensate if a catcher possesses a good arm but not a great arm. Often the difference between a safe or out call lies in getting rid of the ball quickly.

When you have found a catcher who possesses these qualities, the task of teaching him certain fundamentals may be relatively easy.

FUNDAMENTAL CATCHING SKILLS

Like all positions, catching requires certain fundamental skills that must be perfected if the catcher wants to be effective.

Stance

A catcher must have two basic stances: one is for giving signs, and the other is for receiving the pitch. You want the catcher to be in the same position whether or not there are men on base. This keeps him ready for bunts or any slow rollers out in front of the plate and enables him to jump out quickly, ready for the play.

Stance When Giving Signs

The first concern of a catcher is to make sure that no one from the opposing team can see his sign. The catcher assumes his stance by squatting down and putting his weight on the balls of his feet. His left wrist rests on his left knee, with the back of his glove facing the third-base line. This is to prevent the third-base coach from seeing his sign. His right knee points toward the pitcher. His right hand, palm in, is placed on the inside of his thigh just to the right of the crotch. This prevents the first-base coach from seeing the sign. (See Photo 6.1.) After he gives the sign, the catcher goes into his stance for receiving the pitch.

Stance When Receiving the Pitch

The catcher must get as close to the batter as he can without interfering with his swing. He should almost be able to touch the batter's back elbow with his glove. The catcher positions himself so that he can receive the ball and get out as quickly as possible. His feet are slightly

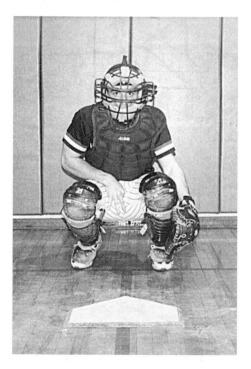

PHOTO 6.1

PHOTO 6.2

more than shoulder width apart, with the toe of his right foot on a line with the ball of his left foot. He is on the balls of his feet. He must have good balance so that he can move quickly.

The stance should be comfortable, not allowing his tail to be too high, nor his shoulders too far forward. An awkward stance can create a pelvic strain. If his tail is too low, it restricts lateral movement. His arms should be relaxed and away from his body, elbows outside knees. (See Photo 6.2.)

The catcher's glove is the pitcher's target and should be placed where the catcher wants the ball. His hand should be relaxed. He keeps his bare hand just behind the thumb part of the glove, with the thumb touching the index finger in a relaxed manner. If a catcher uses a hinged glove, he can keep his hand behind his back when there are no runners on base.

Receiving and Throwing

When getting ready to receive the pitch, the catcher gets as close to the batter as he can. He should be in his stance, giving a good target. He must be aware that he wants the umpire to get a good look at every pitch thrown. A good receiver is smooth and fluid, making as few motions as possible. When he receives the ball, he gives slightly with his hands as he catches the ball.

The toughest part of the job is catching the pitch in the dirt. When this situation occurs, he should drop to his knees, with his glove in the middle. This position keeps the shin guards to be out of the way and places the soft part of the catcher's body in good position to block the ball. His mask and chin are in tight to his body, and he looks at the ball all the way. The shoulders and body are square so that if the ball hits him, it will bounce out in front of him. (See Photo 6.3.) When receiving a pitch from the knees up, he catches the ball with the fingers up and the heel of the glove down. If the pitch is lower, he catches the ball with the fingers down and the heel of the glove up.

When the catcher throws the ball to a base, his body should be balanced, unless a bunt or slow roller requires a quick throw to get the runner. He uses an overhand delivery, gripping the ball across the four seams. The release must be a quick, short, snappy type. The throw is made from the shoulder and is not a complete sweep of the arm.

To throw, the catcher shifts his weight to his back foot and rotates his shoulders to the right while he brings the ball back over his right shoulder. (See Photo 6.4.) He keeps his eyes on the target, cocks his arm just back of the ear, and completes his throw as quickly as possible. He releases the ball with a vigorous wrist and arm snap while pushing off his right foot onto his left foot.

The catcher's footwork, the manner in which he shifts his body into the throw, determines his effectiveness. By shifting his body correctly, he will have rhythm, power, and speed to get rid of the ball in a hurry.

Shifting the Body

A good example of proper shifting of the body is seen in a catcher's ability to step correctly and throw when catching either an inside or an outside pitch. When the ball is to his bare hand or right side, the catcher steps with his right foot first. On pitches to his glove or left side, he steps with his left foot first. Catchers should practice this until it becomes automatic.

PHOTO 6.3   **PHOTO 6.4**

The catcher must be squarely in front of the pitch. He should go into the ball, not catch the ball flat-footed. His weight must be slightly forward.

Framing

A very important skill for a catcher to master is that of *framing*. The umpire's strike zone for the pitcher can be increased through proper framing. The important point here is the catcher's hand or glove position. The glove should always curl toward the strike zone, not away from it. Remember: we are saying a curl or slight turn of the wrist toward the strike zone, not a quick pull or jerking motion. On high pitches, fingers curl down (see Photo 6.5); on outside or inside pitches, the glove hand turns in (see photos 6.6 and 6.7); and on low pitches, the hand and fingers curl up (see Photo 6.8). This technique is practiced whenever the catcher is receiving, whether in the bull pen or during batting practice. It must become a natural technique.

Tagging the Runner

Tag plays at the plate can be of two types. The first is when a runner slides into home plate, and the second is when the runner tries to bowl the catcher over in attempting to jar the ball loose. The catcher must make sure that he faces the runner so that his equipment will protect him. When the catcher lines up the throw coming in, he plants his left foot on the front part of home plate and shows the runner the outside part of home plate so that the runner

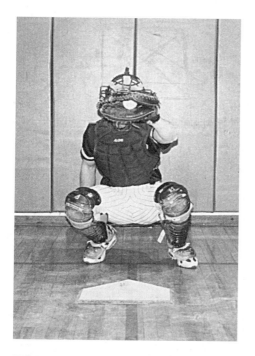

PHOTO 6.5

PHOTO 6.6

PHOTO 6.7

PHOTO 6.8

will slide toward it, not run into him. When he receives the ball, the catcher should hold it with his bare hand, which is in the glove, and tag the runner with the back of the glove. If the runner tries to hit him, he holds the ball in his bare hand, which is in the glove, and tags him with a slight give as contact is made. Otherwise if the catcher stands still and flat-footed, the runner will knock him over.

On force plays at the plate, the catcher receives the ball in front of him, with his right foot on the plate so that he can throw the ball quickly without taking an extra step. The main thing is to stretch out and reach the ball as quickly as possible.

The Pop-Up

Learning how to catch pop-ups requires a lot of hard practice. When the ball is popped up behind home plate, the spin of the ball generally takes it back toward the infield. The catcher should have his back toward the diamond so that the ball will come toward him, rather than away from him. When the ball is popped up, the catcher removes his mask, locates the ball, and then throws his mask away, far enough that he doesn't trip over it. He should try to catch the ball with his glove up, as an outfielder does. On pop-ups in front of the plate and up the infield foul lines, basic priorities prevail. Drills with the coach hitting fungos over the shoulders of the catcher and calling "Left" or "Right" help teach catchers how to turn.

Fielding Bunts

When fielding bunts, the catcher must move out after the ball as quickly as possible. He should field all rolling bunts with two hands, placing the glove out in front of the ball and scooping the ball into the glove with his throwing hand.

The catcher must have good control of the ball before he throws it and must never take his eyes off the ball until he is ready to throw it. If the catcher has time, he should throw the ball overhand; if he does not have time, he has to throw it sidearm, which is like a quick-releasing infield throw.

TIPS FOR CATCHERS

- Be the leader; take charge; be the quarterback.
- Check your infielders to see whether they are in position.
- Be sure to give the pitcher a good target.
- On the intentional pass, keep one foot in the catcher's box until the pitcher releases the ball.
- Learn your pitcher's most effective pitch.
- Always be alert for any steal or hit-and-run situation.
- Back up first base with the bases unoccupied on all batted balls that might result in overthrows.
- Be sure to call "Cut" if you want a ball cut off.
- If a bunt is in order, call for high pitches.
- Study the hitter's stance, and remember what he went after and where he hit the ball in previous at bats.
- Make the signs simple and understandable.

Checklist for Catchers

Stance

_____ Has good signal position, keeping glove hand over left knee and signaling hand inside right thigh.

_____ Is in semierect receiving position, for left or right shift and for readiness to throw.

Receiving and Throwing

_____ Gets as close to the batter as possible when ready to receive the pitch.

_____ Knows proper method of catching pitch in dirt.

_____ Has mastered the art of *framing,* with the glove curling toward the strike zone rather than away from it.

Catching the Ball

_____ Uses two hands.

_____ Brings ball toward the middle of body.

_____ Blocks bad pitches.

_____ Protects throwing hand.

Throwing

_____ Gets ball away quickly.

_____ Takes minimum number of steps.

_____ Throws overhand with quick, snappy release.

_____ Knows where and how to throw on double steal.

Other

_____ Gives signals effectively.

_____ Knows proper way to tag.

_____ Catches foul and fair fly balls.

_____ Fields bunts.

_____ Hustles to back up first base when necessary.

_____ Returns ball to pitcher.

_____ Knows pitchout procedure.

_____ Knows pickoff procedure.

_____ Studies hitters.

_____ Sets up hitters.

_____ Calls play in bunt situation.

Drills for Catchers

DRILL 6.1.   Stance Drill

Purpose: To acquaint the catcher with the proper stance and positions used during the game.

Area Required: Small area of gymnasium or baseball field.

Equipment Needed: Catcher's gear.

Procedure: The coaching staff acquaints the catcher with the proper body positions: feet shoulder width apart, toes pointed straight ahead or slightly toed in, knees pointed straight ahead, and backside low with the back leaning slightly forward. The staff must also teach proper arm, hand, and finger location.

DRILL 6.2.   Signal-Giving Stance

Purpose: To ensure that signs can be seen by the pitcher but not by the opposing team.

Area Required: Part of field or small indoor area.

Equipment Needed: Catcher's gear.

Procedure: Select members of the team to try to pick off the catcher's signals. The coach tells the catcher what signal to give to the pitcher. The pitcher tells an assistant coach or another pitcher what the signal was. The coach makes sure there is agreement.

DRILL 6.3.   Gripping and Throwing Drill

Purpose: To teach the catcher how to grip the ball properly. The ball should be gripped across the seams at the widest part.

Area Required: Small area indoors or on the field.

Equipment Needed: Baseballs.

Procedure: Whenever the catcher is playing catch, he grips the ball quickly across the seams. While catching, he can check his grip and try to increase the speed required for a good release.

DRILL 6.4.   Blocking Drill

Purpose: To teach proper techniques for blocking balls in the dirt.

Area Required: Small space indoors or on the field.

Equipment Needed: Catcher's gear, plastic or Incrediballs.

Procedure: First phase: Position catcher behind plate. Place three balls in front of the plate and point to the one you want blocked. Observe and correct the catcher's response and body position. Repeat as often as necessary. Second phase: Toss balls underhand to various locations, observing and correcting the catcher's reactions. Third phase: Use a fungo to bat balls to the catcher. You can first use the Incrediball and then a baseball.

DRILL 6.5. Dirt-Blocking Drill (Crawl-Walk-Run)

Purpose: To teach the catcher how to get his body to block the baseball. **The catcher learns the technique before using a real baseball.**

Area Required: Small indoor area or plate area on field.

Equipment Needed: Catcher's gear, soft Incrediballs, fungo, and baseballs.

1. Crawl-dry block: The ball is placed on the ground. The coach, assistant, or another catcher calls "Right," "Center," "Left." The coach points to location-reaction time, and the catcher positions himself accordingly. Review basic techniques.
2. Walk-form block: Using the soft Incrediballs, make live throws to build confidence. Tell the catcher the type of pitch; add baseballs when he is ready. Critique his technique.
3. Run-mix block: The coach or ball thrower moves back and gives the catcher a chance to recognize the pitch. This part of the drill deals with the decision-making ability of the catcher; the reaction time is about one-tenth of a second to decide to catch, pick, or block the thrown ball. Stress concentration.
4. All out run-ultimate block-the catcher is challenged: The range of the catcher is expanded to the outside of both batters' boxes through the throws of the coach.

DRILL 6.6. Catchers' Combination Drill

Purpose: To teach blocking, framing, and throwing mechanics in game simulation.

Area Required: 4-foot-wide area, 45 feet long.

Equipment Needed: Full catching gear, catcher's mitt, and one baseball.

Procedure: The catcher must start every sequence in his receiving or secondary stance. The coach or player stands 45 feet away from the catcher. The coach has the option of throwing a marginal strike, dirt ball, or strike. If he throws the ball and does not say anything, the catcher frames the pitch. If he throws the ball in the dirt, the catcher must block and recover. If the coach throws the ball and says "Runner," the catcher must come out of the shoot using the proper footwork for the location of the pitch.

DRILL 6.7. Catchers' Throwing Drill

Purpose: To teach proper arm action, keeping head still, and picking up second without jerking the head.

Area Required: Indoor throwing area or infield.

Equipment Needed: "L" screen, baseballs, and catching gear.

Procedure: The coach throws a pitch to the catcher, who throws to second base. The long end of the "L" screen is placed on the throwing side of the catcher. When the catcher throws the ball to second, if he gets his throwing hand too close to his ear or past the perpendicular, his throw will hit the "L" screen, which is in front of him, about 10 feet away from the plate.

DRILL 6.8.   Get-A-Way Drill

Purpose: To teach the pitcher to field a bunted ball and help the catcher locate a passed ball while the pitcher covers home plate.

Area Required: Mound-to-home plate area or indoor area.

Equipment Needed: Baseballs, bat, and catcher's gear.

Procedure: Two pitchers are on the mound, one behind the other; the catcher is behind the plate in full gear; and a bunter is at the plate. The coach places a passed ball on first base, third base, straight back, or under the catcher. The lead pitcher fields a bunt and throws to first base. The second pitcher points to the ball designated by the coach as a passed ball, and the catcher retrieves the ball and tosses it to the second pitcher, who is covering home plate.

DRILL 6.9.   Fielding Bunted Balls

Purpose: To instruct the catcher in the proper movements for fielding a bunted ball and to acquaint him with his responsibility to take charge.

Area Required: Baseball diamond, either indoors or outdoors.

Equipment Needed: Baseballs, bat, and catcher's gear.

Procedure: The coach or catcher rolls the ball up the first- or third-base line. The coach can stand behind the catcher so that the catcher cannot anticipate the throw and must react. The catcher fields the ball properly and throws to first base. The coach corrects mechanics. When the second baseman, third baseman, and shortstop are added, the coach rolls or bunts the ball, and the catcher will direct players, using verbal and visual signals or methods. The coach makes corrections.

DRILL 6.10.   Backing Up Third

Purpose: To show how it is the catcher's responsibility to move to third when there is a sacrifice bunt and the third baseman has fielded it.

Area Required: Baseball diamond, either indoors or outdoors.

Equipment Needed: Baseball, bat, and catcher's gear.

Procedure: When the coach or bunter hits the ball toward third and the catcher sees the third baseman fielding the bunt, the catcher runs to cover third base. This keeps the runner at first base from advancing to third base.

DRILL 6.11.   Movement When Ball Is in Dirt

Purpose: To block the ball and keep it in front of catcher and under control.

Area Required: Small indoor area or plate area on field.

Equipment Needed: Catching gear, baseballs, and fungo.

Procedure:
1. Catcher is in full gear.
2. Coach or another catcher or pitcher stands about 35 feet away.
3. Ball is thrown* into dirt in front of catcher.
4. Catcher drops to both knees (shin guards are now out of way).
5. Catcher places glove in middle and uses soft part of body to keep ball in front of him.
6. Catcher tries to keep his body square to pitcher (shoulders and body).

DRILL 6.12.   Movement When Ball Is in Dirt (directly in front, runner or runners on base)

Purpose: To try to catch the ball cleanly.

Area Required: Small indoor area or plate area on field.

Equipment Needed: Catching gear, baseballs, and fungo.

Procedure: This is the same as the previous drill, except that the catcher tries to catch the ball before it hits dirt. If he should miss, his body will still be in proper blocking position. The second part of the drill is to have the catcher come up throwing on all fielded balls. The coach makes corrections.

DRILL 6.13.   Blocking Balls in the Dirt to the Right or Left

Purpose: To teach a catcher to move the leg on the side of the bad throw first.

Area Required: Small indoor area or plate area on field.

Equipment Needed: Catching gear, baseballs, and fungo.

Procedure: This is the same as the previous drill, except that throws are to the right or the left. The catcher moves the leg on the side of the bad throw first. The movements

---

*Fungo can also be used at a slightly longer distance—up to 60 feet.

of blocking and trying to catch the ball are used in this drill as well. The coach corrects the glove position. The back hand is used in this drill.

DRILL 6.14.   Dropping the Third Strike

Purpose: To have the catcher and first baseman work together in getting the ball to first base with the least obstruction possible.

Area Required: Indoor or outdoor foul line facsimile.

Equipment Needed: Catching gear and baseballs.

Procedure: The catcher either drops a pitched ball or pretends to do so. His first reaction is to pick up the ball and tag the batter, if possible. His second reaction is to make the first baseman aware of where the catcher is throwing the ball—inside or outside. In most cases, this depends on where the ball has rolled after the catcher drops the third strike. Again, it is important for the catcher and players to know when they are required to throw the batter out at first base. Oral communication is essential in this drill.

DRILL 6.15.   Dropping the Third Strike, Second Drill

Purpose: To teach the catcher to find the dropped third strike and throw properly to first base.

Area Required: Indoor or outdoor foul line facsimile.

Equipment Needed: Catching gear and baseballs.

Procedure: The coach or pitcher throws the ball to the catcher. He catches the ball and looks to the coach's hand to see where ball is. The catcher reacts by turning in the direction of the ball, finding it, and throwing to first base. As he throws, he lets the first baseman know whether the throw is inside or outside. The coach instructs in proper fundamentals and makes the necessary corrections.

DRILL 6.16.   Force Play

Purpose: To teach the catcher proper footwork when he catches a ball at the plate in a force-out situation.

Area Required: Home plate with first-base foul line.

Equipment Needed: Catching gear and baseballs.

Procedure: The coach stands 25–30 feet from the catcher. He throws a baseball to the plate. The catcher catches the ball with his right foot on the plate. As he receives the throw, he steps with his left foot and throws the ball back to the first baseman.

DRILL 6.17. Pop-ups

Purpose: To acquaint the catcher with placing back to the diamond when the ball is ball hit over his head and with discarding his mask.

Area Required: Indoor or home plate area.

Equipment Needed: Catching gear, baseballs, and fungo or tennis racquet.

Procedure: The coach hits the ball behind the catcher with a fungo or reinforced tennis racquet. The catcher turns and locates the ball, then discards his mask when the ball is at its greatest height. The ball is caught with the glove in the middle of his forehead. The coach comments on correct mechanics and reactions.

Equipment needed to hit pop-up:

1. Tennis racquet with rubber ball.
2. Pitching machine.

DRILL 6.18. Timing and Accuracy

Purpose: To time the catcher's throws to second base and grade accuracy.

Area Required: Infield area.

Equipment Needed: Baseballs, radar gun, and stopwatches.

Procedure: Each catcher is in full catcher's gear and throws five times to second base, with another catcher standing in right-hand or left-hand part of the batter's box. Each catcher throws three balls with right-hand batter and two with left-hand batter standing at the plate. Pitchers on the mound throw two pitches to the plate for every pickoff at first base. Alternate so that the catcher will not know when the pitcher is throwing to the plate.

Middle infielders alternate at second base, working on footwork on steals at second and receiving the throw from the catcher. The first basemen alternate at first base, receiving pickoff throws from the pitcher and yelling, "There he goes!" All pitchers feed from the third-base line, one at a time. All other position players are at first base, stealing second base two at a time and working on their stealing leads and breaks to second base. The runners do not go all the way to second base but run at full speed to about 30 feet from the bag. They also should work on looking in on steal attempts.

This is an excellent drill for catchers' throws, pitchers' pickoff moves, and slide steps to first; first basemen fielding picks at first and communicating on steals; middle infielders working on footwork and tags at second base; and conditioning and baserunning skill improvement. (See Figure 6.1.)

CATCHERS' THROWING CHART

ACCURACY GRADE: 1 pt. – Noncatchable ball (dirt or air)
2 pts – Catchable but off line (dirt or air)
3 pts. – Catchable dirt ball
4 pts. – Catchable on bag (high)
5 pts. – Perfect throw

NAME (DATE)	TIME		ACCURACY		GUN TIMES	
	RHB	LHB	RHB	LHB	RHB	LHB
1.						
2.						
3.						
4.						
5.						
1.						
2.						
3.						
4.						
5.						
1.						
2.						
3.						
4.						
5.						
1.						
2.						
3.						
4.						
5.						
1.						
2.						
3.						
4.						
5.						

7

THE FUNDAMENTALS
OF INFIELD PLAY

Infield play is a mechanical part of the game and can be improved by constant practice. To develop strong infield play, you must instruct your players in both the mental and the physical aspects of the game. An infielder must think about what he will do with the ball if it is hit to him. He must know the score, the number of outs, the number of men on base, the inning, which hitter is up in the lineup, and so on.

WHAT INFIELDERS MUST KNOW

Knowledge of the Hitter

The infielder should look at the hitter in the batter's box and determine to the best of his ability what type of hitter he appears to be. The infielder may have seen the hitter play before, he may have seen a scouting report on him, or he may use simple deductions to get his information.

If the hitter is the leadoff hitter and small in stature, the infielder can assume that he is a fast runner, is probably a good bunter, and does not have much power. If he is the number three or four hitter, the infielder can assume that he might be a pull hitter, has some home run power, and so on. The infielder should look at the hitter's stance and the way he holds the bat to get an indication of what type of hitter he is and then determine how he is going to play him.

Knowledge of Playing Conditions

The infielder should check his position thoroughly before the game. He should check to see whether the ground is hard, soft, fast, slow, wet, or dry. Is the grass high or low, or is it a skin infield with no grass? He should check the sun to see whether it will affect fly balls or line drives. He should continue to monitor the sun during the whole game. Will the wind have any effect on fly balls during the game?

Anticipating the Play

The infielder should watch the catcher relay the signs to the pitcher so that he will know what pitch will be thrown and can position himself accordingly. He should know the number of outs, the score, the inning, what hitter in the lineup is at bat, and the game situation. He should be alert for hit-and-run situations, bunt situations, straight or delayed steal situations, and so on. The infielder must always be alert and should never be taken by surprise.

BASIC INFIELDER'S STANCE

The stance for the infielder is comfortable and relaxed. His feet are approximately shoulder width apart. His left foot is slightly in front of his right foot. His weight is evenly distributed on the balls of the feet. His body faces the hitter squarely. His hands are resting on his knees, which are slightly bent, and he watches the pitcher. This is the *relaxed* position.

From the relaxed position he must get himself to the *ready* position. As the pitcher starts his windup, the infielder removes his hands from his knees and takes a short jab step with the left foot and then the right foot, toward home plate. He does this to get his body in motion before the ball is hit. While taking the short jab steps toward home plate, he is following the flight of the ball from the pitcher's hand to home plate. The infielder is now in the ready position.

Another way to get to the ready position is to pick up his feet in a continuous motion as the pitcher starts his windup, rather than taking the short jab steps. This is similar to the way in which a tennis player prepares himself to receive a serve. (See Photo 7.1.)

CATCHING, THROWING, AND FIELDING SKILLS

Catching a Thrown Ball

The fielder should always catch a thrown ball with two hands, and he should try to be directly in front of it when he catches it. His hands are extended away from his body, with a slight bend at the elbows. When the ball is in his glove, his hands should give (*soft hands*) and be brought into his body or into the throwing area.

To catch a ball above the waist, his palms are turned away from his body, and his hands are placed in a position we call *thumb to thumb.* To catch a ball below the waist, his palms face upward, hands placed in a position we call *pinky to pinky.*

Throwing the Ball

An infielder must be able to throw the ball from all positions. After fielding the ball, the infielder brings the ball to the center of his body (belt), separates the ball from the glove, and gets the ball into throwing position. His front shoulder points directly toward the player to

PHOTO 7.1

whom he is throwing. Pointing his front toe, he steps with his stride leg directly toward the same player. As the stride leg lands, his arm starts to come through and the upper part of his body should be square to the receiving player. We call this the *four corners* position. The tops of both shoulders and the points of both hips are squarely facing the player who is to receive the ball. As the ball is released, the infielder should have a good follow-through. This helps get velocity into the throw, and it improves his accuracy.

The infielder should grip the ball across the wide seams on the ball *(four-seam rotation)*. The four-seam rotation keeps the trajectory of the ball in a straight line and makes it easier for the waiting receiver to catch it.

Fielding a Ground Ball Hit Directly at the Infielder

When the ball is hit directly at the infielder, from his ready position he should take his first step with the right foot to position his body to the right of the ball. This is because the most difficult ball for an infielder is a medium-speed ground ball hit directly at him. This kind of hit does not give him the opportunity to read the speed and hops of the ball. When he is to the right of the ball, he has a better angle for judging these things.

The infielder approaches the ball with his body low and under control, keeping his eyes on the ball, not looking at the runner. He places his body in front of the ball. As he catches the ball, his left foot is slightly in front of the his right foot, hands away from his body, and he looks the ball into the glove. He fields the ball just inside his left foot, with the glove and throwing hand together, pinky to pinky, and his arms slightly bent, forming a *V* leading to the shoulders. The glove, arms, and shoulders are considered a triangle in good fielding form.

As the infielder catches the ball, his hands give slightly, and he separates the ball from the glove as quickly as possible to get it into the throwing area. The infielder takes a skip step or crow hop to get himself into good throwing position. He steps directly toward the fielder receiving the throw and throws overhand whenever possible.

Fielding a Ground Ball Hit to the Left of the Infielder

From the ready stance, the infielder uses the crossover step, pivots on the left foot, crosses over with the right foot, and gets his body in front of the ball. He fields the ball just inside his left foot.

To get into position to throw while going left, the infielder must use a *cross-back step*. This means that as he fields the ball just off the inside of his left foot, he crosses his right foot behind his left and plants it. This stops his momentum and turns his body in the direction in which he is throwing. He steps with his left foot in that direction, opens up his body to show the four corners, and follows through on the throw.

Fielding a Ground Ball Hit to the Right of the Infielder

From the ready position, the infielder uses the crossover step. He pivots on his right foot, crosses over with his left, and slides his body in front of the ball. He fields the ball just inside his left foot and plants his right foot hard into the ground to stop his momentum. He then takes a skip step and throws. If the runner is fast, the infielder may not have time to take the skip step, and he may have to throw with no step. If the infielder has to backhand the ball, he should try to plant his right foot and get rid of the ball as quickly as possible.

Fielding a Slow Hit Ball

The infielder charges the ball and, as he approaches it, gets his body under control. His body is approximately one step to the right of the ball. This gives him a better angle for throwing. He fields the ball with his glove as he comes across the ball. He then steps forward with his right foot and throws underhand off his right foot. The only time he should field the ball with his bare hand is when the ball is dead in the grass or almost completely stopped.

Recovering a Bobbled Ball

When an infielder bobbles a ball, he should not panic. He must remain calm, locate the ball, and get to it as quickly as possible. He picks the ball up with his bare hand because he has more control of that hand than of the glove hand. After he picks up the ball, he does not put it back into the glove. He brings the hand and the ball to the throwing area immediately.

To pick up the ball with his bare hand, the infielder uses his hand as a *three-pronged tool.* The prongs are the index, middle, and ring fingers. The thumb and pinky go to the other side of the ball. The infielder *pushes* the ball into the ground. He should not try to get his fingers under the ball. Actually, he is going after the ball with three fingers and coming up to throw with two fingers.

GENERAL INFIELD POSITIONING

Normal Depth

This is where the infielder plays most hitters. He changes his position according to the game situation or a left- or right-handed hitter. (See Figure 7.1.)

Infield Halfway

This is double-play positioning. The shortstop and second baseman move approximately 8–10 feet in from their normal position and 8–10 feet closer to second base. The first and third basemen are approximately 5–8 feet behind the base. If there is no runner on second base, the first baseman holds the runner. It is also possible to make a play on a runner at home plate if the ball is hit sharply and directly toward an infielder.

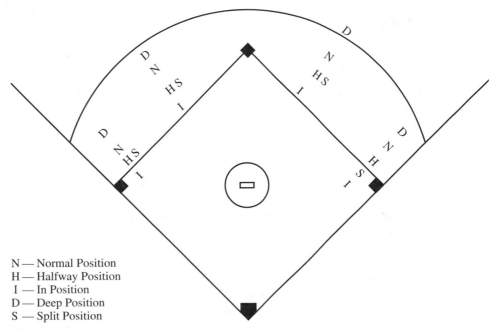

N — Normal Position
H — Halfway Position
I — In Position
D — Deep Position
S — Split Position

FIGURE 7.1

Infield In

This position is usually at the edge of the infield grass. The infielder should be ready to make the out at home plate. This is the most precarious position for the infielder because it limits his range, and balls hit hard, not directly at a fielder, usually find their way into the outfield.

Infield Deep

All infielders play as deep as possible. The shortstop and second baseman play on the edge of the grass, or deeper if the speed of the runner allows it. The first and third basemen should be 15–20 feet behind the bases. The infielders are trying to get more range and keep the ball in the infield.

Split Infield

The shortstop and second baseman are at double-play depth, and the first and third basemen play even with the bases. From this position, the shortstop and second baseman can make a play at home plate or go for the double play. The first and third basemen have the same options.

THE FIRST BASEMAN

Qualifications

- Tall, agile, strong, quick hands and feet.
- Able to field ground balls and take throws.
- Preferably left-handed.

Positioning

- Deep. The first baseman normally plays at the edge of the outfield grass and wide of the base. This enables him to cover the most ground.
- Halfway. The first baseman moves halfway between the outfield grass and first base. This position is used when there is a slight possibility of a bunt or there is a hitter at home plate with better than average speed.
- Holding the runner on. The first baseman takes a position to hold the runner on any time second base is unoccupied, unless the game situation dictates otherwise.
- Bunt situation. The first baseman holds the runner on base with second base unoccupied. He breaks toward home plate with the pitch. With second base occupied, the first baseman plays two steps on the grass, not holding the runner, and charges toward home plate with the pitch.

Catching the Ball

Catching thrown balls is the primary job of the first baseman. He catches the ball with two hands whenever possible.

For a ball that is thrown to the infield side of first base, a right-handed first baseman shifts his feet to the inside of the base and touches the base with his right foot. A left-handed first baseman touches first base with his left foot, crosses over with his right, and reaches for the ball with his glove hand.

For a throw to the outfield side of first base, a right-handed first baseman touches first base with his right foot, crosses over with his left, and reaches for the ball with his glove hand. A left-handed first baseman shifts his feet, touches the base with his left foot, and reaches for the ball with the glove hand.

Catching Balls Thrown in the Dirt

The general rule for balls in the dirt is to make sure that the first baseman blocks the ball. He must not let the ball get by and let the runner advance another base.

Scoop (Short Hop)

The first baseman stretches to reach the ball. A right-handed first baseman keeps his right foot in contact with the base. A left-handed first baseman keeps his left foot in contact with the base. The first baseman tries to catch the ball at the closest point of contact with the ground. He should not stretch until the ball is released by the other infielder. By stretching too soon, the first baseman cuts down on his ability to move or shift with the throw.

Long Hop

The first baseman keeps his body erect and lets the ball come to him on the big hop. He does not stretch for the ball.

In-between Hop

The first baseman backs up slightly, shoulders hunched over and weight slightly forward. He stays on the infield side of the base and makes sure that he blocks the ball with his body.

Catching the High Throw

The first baseman steps on the top of the base to get added height as he receives the throw. A right-handed first baseman steps on the base with his right foot; the left-handed first baseman with his left foot. After receiving the throw, the first baseman steps into foul territory to avoid a collision with the runner.

Leaving the Base to Catch a Throw

If the first baseman cannot keep his foot on the base and reach the ball, he must get off the base so that the ball does not get past him. If the throw is to the inside of the diamond (up the first-base line), the first baseman should come off the base and try to make a sweeping tag on the runner as he goes by.

Fielding

Throwing to Second Base

During infield practice, the first baseman makes the play as he would during a game. A left-handed first baseman throws from where he fields the ball. A right-handed first baseman turns inside toward second base, straightens up, and throws. The first baseman never turns his back to the infield.

All throws to second base should be made quickly. It is not how hard the ball is thrown, but the speed and accuracy that count. The lead runner must be retired to ensure the double play. The first baseman always throws at the shortstop's face.

If the first baseman is playing deep behind first base, his throw is to the outside (outfield) side of second base. If he is playing in or holding the runner on, his throw is to the inside (infield) side of the base.

Feeding the Ball to the Pitcher Covering First Base

When the first baseman fields a ground ball to first base, he makes the play unassisted whenever possible. Only when he cannot beat the runner to the base does he make the play to the pitcher covering. The throw is a soft, underhand, stiff-wristed toss about chest high. The ball is fielded, and the first baseman moves toward first base. He takes the ball out of his glove and tosses it to the pitcher just before he reaches first base. If the pitcher receives the ball before reaching the base, the only thing he has to be concerned about is touching the base. If he receives the ball as he reaches the base, he must catch the ball, touch the base, and avoid the runner.

Positioning with Runners on Base

- Runner on first base only: The first baseman holds the runner on in this case. His right foot is on the inside corner of first base. His body is angled to receive a pickoff throw from the pitcher. As the pitcher delivers the ball to home plate, the first baseman steps into the diamond with his left foot and crosses over with the right. This puts him in a position squarely facing home plate. He is now in position to react to any ball hit in his direction.
- Runners on first and second (bunt situation): The first baseman plays on the edge of the infield grass, not holding the runner on. He charges toward home plate with the pitch and looks to make the play at third base. The catcher makes the call in this situation.
- Runners on first and second (no bunt situation): The first baseman plays behind the runner and is ready to make a double play (3-6-3 or 3-6-1).

Tagging

Tagging is much easier for a left-handed first baseman because his glove hand is closer to first base. A right-handed first baseman must reach across his body to make a tag, which should be quick and sweeping. The glove is swept across the inside portion of first base.

Pop Flies

The first baseman calls for the ball. He takes charge on all balls hit between the catcher and the first baseman and also between the pitcher and the first baseman. On foul balls near the stands or fence, the first baseman must get to the fence first and then, if necessary, he can drift back toward the infield. If he drifts toward the fence, he will be looking for the fence and can lose sight of the ball.

Topped Balls

On all topped balls in fair territory in front of home plate, the first baseman gives his target in fair territory. He places his left foot on first base and stretches into the diamond. On a passed ball in foul territory (first-base line), he gives his target in foul territory. He places his right foot on the base and stretches into foul territory.

Cutoffs

The first baseman is the cutoff man on all balls hit to center field and right field. On those that are sure doubles or possible triples, the first baseman steps inside the diamond to make sure that the runner touches first base. He then follows the runner to second base in case the runner rounds it. If the ball is cut off and thrown behind the runner at second base, the first baseman makes the play.

Fielding Bunts

With a runner on first base, the first baseman must hold the runner on. When the pitcher delivers the ball to home plate, the first baseman charges and has the responsibility of fielding any bunt along the first-base line. He must listen to the catcher, who determines where the throw will be made. Remember: you must get an out in this situation.

With runners on first and second bases, the first baseman positions himself 10–15 feet in front of first base on the infield grass. He charges as the pitcher delivers the ball to home plate, and he must field any ball bunted along the first-base line or behind the pitcher. He listens for the catcher to tell him where to throw.

TIPS FOR FIRST BASEMEN

- Never play so far from the base as to require extra effort to reach the base before a thrown ball arrives.
- Be quick with the first three or four steps. Ninety percent of the balls fielded by the first baseman are within the three- or four-step range.
- Move toward the ball on grounders coming straight at you. Keep your body low and your hands close to the ground. It is easier to raise your hands than to lower them.
- Make the play unassisted whenever possible.
- Your primary duty is to catch a thrown ball, even if you have to leave the base to do it.
- Practice catching with the glove hand from all angles, but use two hands whenever possible.
- In taking a throw from another infielder, run to the base, touch it with one foot, and assume the straddle position. You can shift left or right to catch the ball and still have a foot on the base.

- Two good rules to follow on a ball hit to the right of first base: If it's hot, take a shot. If it's slow, let it go.
- Get off the base to block an errant throw. Do not let it get by.
- Generally play 15–20 feet behind the base and 10 feet from the foul line. This will vary depending on the quickness of the first baseman.
- For right-handed hitters, play closer to second base; for slow runners, play deeper.
- In fielding a bunt, try to field the ball on your right side so you can pivot and throw quickly. Charge the ball and try to make the out on the lead runner. If in doubt, throw to first base. You must get an out in this situation.
- When the pitcher covers first base, throw the ball softly with an underhand motion. Show the ball to the pitcher.
- Always protect the line in the late innings. A ball hit between the first baseman and the foul line is usually good for extra bases.
- Watch the hitter while the ball is being pitched. The first baseman gets a better jump on the ball and picks up the batter attempting to bunt the ball much faster than if he is watching the ball travel toward home plate.
- Be alert at all times, and constantly practice to improve your weaknesses.

THE THIRD BASEMAN

Qualifications

- Strong, quick hands and feet.
- Sure hands.
- Strong arm and chest; must be able to block ball.

Positioning

- Deep. The third baseman plays as deep and as wide of the base as the hitter allows.
- Normal. The third baseman plays three or four steps in from the deep position and shades the hole toward shortstop unless he is shading the line with an extreme pull hitter batting. He protects the line in the late innings of close games, to keep runners out of scoring position.
- In (bunt situation). The third baseman plays two or three steps in front of third base on the infield grass.
- In (play at plate). The third baseman plays even with the base and charges anything hit at him. He can see the runner as he fields the ball and can determine whether he has a play at the plate.

Fielding Techniques

1. The third baseman blocks all hard-hit balls, trying to keep the play in front of him.
2. On a ball slow hit toward the shortstop, the third baseman cuts in front of the shortstop and makes the play, because he is in motion toward first base. The third baseman never catches this ball if he must leave his feet, because the shortstop may still be able to make the play.

3. With a player who has a tendency to bunt, the third baseman shortens up his position and watches the barrel of the bat.
4. On swinging bunts, the third baseman charges the ball fast. If the ball is still rolling, he fields it with two hands.
   a. The third baseman throws from the position of fielding, with the motion going toward first base.
   b. If the ball has stopped or is rolling very slowly, he fields the ball with his bare hand, keeping his head down and his body low. He cups his hand so that he can get his fingers under the ball. He fields the ball with his left foot forward and throws off the right foot to first base. The throw is underhand and across the body. He aims it to the inside of the diamond because an underhand throw has a tendency to dip and tail into the baseline.
   c. The third baseman never throws if there is no chance to get the runner.

Bunt Situations

1. A man is on first.
   a. When the third baseman is anticipating a sacrifice bunt, he charges in when the pitcher delivers the ball.
   b. When the ball is bunted hard to the third baseman, he fields it and the catcher makes the call.
   c. If the play at second base is doubtful, he gets an out at first base.
2. Men are on first and second bases.
   a. The third baseman's judgement is the key on this play. He is in full command of the play.
   b. The third baseman stands three steps in front of the base and just inside the foul line.
   c. The third baseman tells the pitcher that he must field the ball. Important: he must know the pitcher's fielding ability.
   d. He must get an out in this situation.
   e. On a bunted ball the pitcher can handle easily, the third baseman retreats to the base and takes the throw.
   f. On a ball bunted hard that the pitcher cannot field, the third baseman must charge, field the ball, and get the out at first base.
   g. If the third baseman's judgement is to go for the ball, he should run the pitcher off.
   h. If the third baseman's judgement is wrong and the pitcher fields the ball, a play cannot be made at third base because the base is uncovered. The pitcher must try to get the out at first base.

Pop Flies

1. A pop fly close to the infield area is the third baseman's responsibility. It is his play until he is called off by another infielder.
2. The third baseman takes all pop flies that he can easily reach out in front of home plate.
3. When the pop fly is in foul territory close to the stands, the catcher does not call. If the third baseman can reach the ball, he calls and runs the catcher off the play.

4. The third baseman keeps all foul pop flies near the stands on his right side because the ball comes down from right to left.

Cutoffs

The third baseman is the cutoff man on all throws to home plate from left field. If he is going to let the ball go through to the catcher at home plate, he must fake the cutoff to freeze any other runners on base.

TIPS FOR THIRD BASEMEN

- Always watch the hitter, especially his hands, to see the bat angle and attempted bunts.
- On balls hit directly back to the pitcher, always break toward the middle of the infield so that you are in position to field a deflected ball.
- Always pick up a bobbled ball with your bare hand.

THE SHORTSTOP

Qualifications

Shortstop is the toughest infield position to play. Therefore the shortstop should be your best infielder. He must be agile and have quick reflexes, hands, and feet. The shortstop must have a strong arm in order to make the play deep in the hole. If he does not have a strong arm, he must have the ability to get rid of the ball quickly.

Positioning

- Deep. The shortstop should play as deep as possible to give himself the best chance to reach any ball hit in his direction. He may be able to take a step or two back on the outfield grass if there is a slow runner, or he may have to take a step or two closer to home plate if there is a fast runner at home plate.
- Halfway (double-play position). The shortstop must cheat in toward home plate and closer to second base. A good rule of thumb for determining the cheating position is to move three steps toward home plate and three steps closer to second base. The most important factor involved in the cheating position is that the shortstop must be able to get to the base, set himself, and await the throw. He should not have to receive the throw while running at full speed.
- In. The shortstop plays at the edge of the infield grass, ready to make the play at home plate.

Fielding Techniques

- Ground ball hit to the right. The shortstop, reacting from his ready position, uses the crossover step, moves toward the ball, slides his body in front of the ball, and plants on his right foot. By planting on the right foot, he stops his momentum from going away from where he wants to throw. After planting the right foot, he pushes off, takes a skip step, and throws to first base.

- Ground ball hit to the left. The shortstop, reacting from his ready position, uses the crossover step to get in front of the ball and field it directly in front of his body. After he has fielded the ground ball, he takes a cross-back step to turn his body so he is facing the first baseman as he makes his throw. To execute the *cross-back step,* the shortstop drops his right foot behind his left foot, plants the right foot, and throws to first base.
- The slow-hit ball. The shortstop charges the ball and gets his body under control as he approaches the ball. He circles into the ball if possible. *Circling into the ball* means that as he approaches the ball, he is one step to the right of it. This gives him a better angle from which to throw to first base. He fields the ball with his left foot forward, takes a step with his right foot, and throws underhand, across his body, to first base.

Pop Flies

The shortstop takes all of the pop flies that he can reach in the infield. The shortstop has priority over the third baseman on any pop fly that the third baseman has to back up to catch. The shortstop attempts to catch any pop fly in short left field or center field until called off by one of the outfielders.

THE SECOND BASEMAN

Qualifications

- Quick hands and feet.
- Able to field all types of ground balls quickly.
- Able to pivot on double play.
- Strong arm not crucial (most throws are short).

Positioning

- Deep. The second baseman should give himself the best possible chance to reach any ball hit in the direction of second base. He may be able to take a step or two back on the outfield grass if there is a slow runner at the plate, or he may have to take a step or two closer to home plate if there is a fast runner at the plate. If he is playing on astroturf, he may even be able to play in short right field, because the ball will get to him much more quickly on the turf than on grass.
- Halfway (double play position). The second baseman must cheat in toward home plate and closer to second base, as does that the shortstop.
- In. The second baseman plays on the edge of the infield grass, ready to make the play at home plate.

Fielding Techniques

- Ground ball hit to the right. The second baseman, reacting from his ready position, uses the crossover step, moves toward the ball, slides his body in front of the ball, and plants on his right foot. This stops his momentum from going away from where he wants to throw. After planting the right foot, he pushes off, takes a skip step, and throws to first base.

- Ground ball hit to the left. The second baseman, reacting from his ready position, uses the crossover step to get himself into a position to field the ball directly in front of his body. After he has fielded the ground ball, he takes a cross-back step to turn his body so that he is facing the first baseman as he makes the throw.
- Fielding a slow-hit ball. The second baseman charges the ball and gets his body under control as he approaches the ball. He circles the ball if possible, giving himself a better angle from which to throw to first base. He fields the ball with his left foot forward, takes a step with his right foot, and throws underhand, across his body, to first base.

Pop Flies

The second baseman attempts to catch all pop flies around the second base area and behind first base when the first baseman must back up to catch the ball. He also attempts to catch all pop flies in short center field and right field until he is called off by either the shortstop or one of the outfielders.

TIPS FOR INFIELDERS

- Think ahead.
- Look for the ball to be hit to you on every play.
- Have a comfortable stance.
- Be well balanced.
- Face the hitter squarely.
- Use the crossover step on balls hit to the left and right.
- Have your body under control as you approach the ball.
- Always get at least one out on a ground ball.
- Know your pop-up priorities.
- Do not make any unnecessary throws.
- Hustle after a bobbled ball, and pick it up with your bare hand.
- Give the outfielder a target with your glove when acting as a relay man.

Tagging Runners

1. Time permitting, the infielder straddles the base and receives the throw at a point directly above the base.
2. He lets the runner come to the base, not reaching out to make the tag. If he reaches out, a good slider may evade the tag.
3. The infielder makes all tags with the back of his glove hand.
4. He keeps his hands relaxed.
5. An infielder must be a quick, aggressive tagger and never leave his glove hand down too long. He makes quick, sweeping tags.
6. The infielder ensures that the umpire has called the play before tossing the ball to another player.
7. The infielder never retags. If the tag is missed, the runner still may be called out. If the infielder goes to retag, the umpire knows that he thinks he missed the tag.
8. The infielder is alert for runners oversliding the base while trying to avoid a tag.
9. After making the tag, the infielder is ready to throw to another base for a continuing play.

8

THE DOUBLE PLAY: SIMPLE TECHNIQUES FOR ITS EXECUTION

The double play is the most important play in baseball. Without a good double play combination, a team will not win many close games.

The shortstop and second baseman must be a team within a team. They must know each other's thoughts, reactions, abilities, and shortcomings. In all practices, the shortstop and second baseman should play catch and pepper together, and on road trips they should even room together.

BASIC PRINCIPLES OF THE DOUBLE PLAY

To make the double play, players must follow a few basic principles. First, the double play requires that infielders *cheat* or *shade* the bag. This means that both the shortstop and second baseman must give up ground, moving closer to second base and home plate. A good rule of thumb is to move three steps closer to second base and three steps closer to home plate. This distance varies with the speed of individual infielders. Our feeling is that the double play must be made on a ball hit up the middle. Usually a ball hit in the hole results only in a force at second base. (See Figure 8.1.)

Second, the player who is on the pivot end of the double play must get to the base as quickly as possible. He must approach the base with both hands held chest high, giving his partner a target, and he must have his body under control. In this way, he can adjust and make sure of the first out if the throw is bad. Remember: you cannot make a double play if you do not get the lead man.

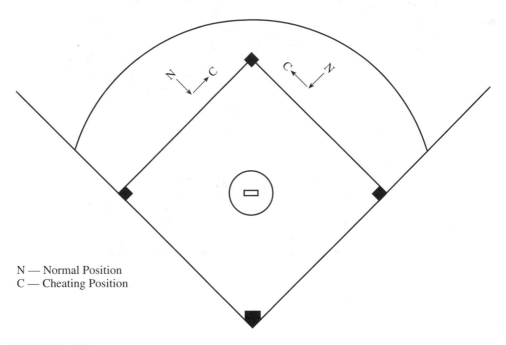

N — Normal Position
C — Cheating Position

FIGURE 8.1

PIVOTS BY THE SHORTSTOP

The shortstop has three basic pivots.

1. The shortstop rounds into the base with his hands held high to give a target to the fielder who is making the initial throw. He has his body under control as he approaches the base. He places his right foot just behind the corner of the base and drags the foot across the base, with his momentum taking him toward first base. (See Photo 8.1.)
2. The shortstop uses the second pivot when taking a throw from the first baseman, who is holding the runner on, or when fielding the ball on the infield grass. The shortstop rounds into the base and gets his body under control with hands held high, but this time he positions himself on the third-base side of second base. When the throw is made, he places his left foot on the inside portion of the base and steps into the infield to complete the throw to first base. (See Photo 8.2.)
3. For the third pivot, the shortstop fields the ball close enough to second base so that he can take the play himself without involving the second baseman. As the shortstop fields the ball, usually within two or three steps from second base, he should have some verbal communication with the second baseman. The shortstop can say, "I've got it," or the second baseman can tell him, "Take it yourself." The shortstop then continues to the base. As he sets up to throw, he places his left foot on the back of the base and throws to first base, using the base as protection between himself and the runner. (See Photo 8.3.)

PHOTO 8.1

PHOTO 8.2

PHOTO 8.3

PIVOTS BY THE SECOND BASEMAN

The pivot from the second-base side is a little more difficult because the second baseman has his back to the runner and cannot see him. Many double plays are incomplete because the second baseman hears footsteps. The second baseman must possess some degree of courage to take the throw and make his throw to first base without worrying about being taken out of the play by a sliding baserunner. For this reason, we suggest teaching a variety of pivots to the second baseman so that no matter where the feed is, he has some means of avoiding the runner.

The first pivot we teach is the one we feel is the easiest for the second baseman to master. It is the pivot that can be used most of the time, and it also takes him away from the path of the runner. The second baseman's approach to the base is the same as that of the shortstop. He must round into the base, hands held high as a target for the shortstop, and must keep his body under control as he approaches the base. As the throw is made, the second baseman is one step behind second base, on the outfield side of the base. He places his right foot to the outfield side of the base and steps over the base with his left foot. As he catches the ball, he drags his right foot across the back corner of the base nearest third base. He should plant on the right foot and throw to first base. (See Photos 8.4 and 8.5.)

For the next pivot, the second baseman places his left foot on top of the base. He catches the ball, comes across the base, plants on his right foot, and throws to first base. (See Photo 8.6.)

For the third pivot, the second baseman places his left foot on the base, receives the ball, and pushes back off the base. He lands, plants on the right foot, and throws to first base. (See Photo 8.7.)

PHOTO 8.4

PHOTO 8.5

PHOTO 8.6

PHOTO 8.7

The fourth pivot is the straddle. (See Photo 8.8.) To use this, a second baseman must have a strong arm. He gets to the base as quickly as possible and straddles the base. As he receives the throw, he touches the front of the base on the first-base side with his left toe and throws to first base. After making the pivot, he must remember not to be a spectator, but to get out of the way of the incoming runner. (See Photo 8.9.)

PHOTO 8.8

PHOTO 8.9

PHOTO 8.10

The last pivot is used on a hard-hit ball, when there is no chance that the runner can take out the second baseman. The second baseman gets to the base as quickly as possible and plants his right foot on the inside portion of the base. (See Photo 8.10.) He receives the ball, pushes off on his right foot, and throws to first base.

FEEDS FROM THE SHORTSTOP

Underhand Toss

The underhand toss is used when the shortstop fields the ball close to second base. He fields the ground ball while moving toward second base, with his left foot forward. As he takes the ball out of his glove, the shortstop pivots on his left foot and steps toward the second baseman with his right foot. He makes the toss while stepping toward the second baseman with his right foot. He takes the ball out of the glove to give the second baseman a good view of the ball.

The shortstop makes the toss, a stiff-wristed, underhand toss, from just off his right hip. He does not let his arm follow through any higher than the shoulder. The toss has no arc to it and is aimed at the second baseman's chest. After tossing the ball, the shortstop continues his forward motion toward second base. (See Photo 8.11.)

PHOTO 8.11   **PHOTO 8.12**

Backhand Toss

The backhand toss is used when the ball is fielded far to the left and behind second base. This is also a stiff-wristed, forearm toss, made while the weight is on the left foot. The toss is aimed at the third-base side of second base, which allows the second baseman to complete his pivot. (See Photo 8.12.)

Sidearm Toss (Open Up)

This toss is used on any ground ball that the shortstop can charge if he can get his body completely in front of it. He fields the ball with his right foot slightly in front of his left foot. This opens his left hip, allowing the toss to be made smoothly. If the ball were fielded with his left foot forward, his left hip would be locked, and the shortstop would have to throw across his body. As the shortstop makes the throw to second base, his weight is on his right foot, and he pivots on the balls of his feet. He does not straighten up. Players just learning this toss can place their right knee on the ground when making the toss. (See Photo 8.13.)

Sidearm Toss (Slide in and Plant)

This toss is used on any ball hit to the shortstop's right when he can get in front of it but cannot charge it. The shortstop gets his body in front of the ball and slides on his right foot, planting it hard into the ground. As he plants his right foot, he opens his left hip and throws right from where he fields the ball to the second baseman. Remember:

PHOTO 8.13

- Open up the left hip to aid in making the throw.
- Do not hide the ball in the glove when making the toss.
- Do not straighten up—stay low.

Backhand Play

After fielding the ball in the backhand position, the shortstop takes one more step with his right foot. He plants on his right foot, opens up his left hip, and throws to second base. He makes sure of an accurate throw to second base because he probably will get only one out on this play.

FEEDS FROM THE SECOND BASEMAN

Underhand Toss

The underhand toss is used on ground balls hit to the right of the second baseman and close to the base. As the second baseman fields the ball in the center of his body, he pivots on his right foot and steps toward the base with his left foot. He takes the ball out of his glove and feeds it to the shortstop with a stiff-wristed, underhand toss. He does not let his arm follow through any higher than the shoulder. The toss does not have any arc to it and is aimed directly at the shortstop's chest. The second baseman continues his forward motion toward second base after releasing the ball. (See Photo 8.14.)

PHOTO 8.14

Backhand Flip

The backhand flip can be used instead of the underhand toss. It should be used only on a ball hit to the second baseman's right and only if he can get his body directly in front of it. He makes the toss from no more than 20 feet from second base. This is also a stiff-wristed, forearm flip. He takes the ball out of his glove and feeds it to the shortstop with his elbow and hand parallel to the ground. The palm of the hand is facing the shortstop. He pushes the ball in a backhand manner toward the shortstop's chest. The ball has very little or no spin and no arc. After tossing the ball, the second baseman continues his motion toward second base to complete the follow-through. This continuation of his motion improves the accuracy of the toss. (See Photo 8.15.)

Jump Turn

This feed is used when the second baseman is too far from second base to use the underhand toss or backhand flip. He fields the ground ball directly in front of his body with two hands. (See Photo 8.16.) As he catches it, he turns his entire body toward second base by means of a jump. As he jumps, he plants on his right foot and throws to second base. He does not straighten up, but stays low to throw. The throw is the same as for throwing a dart—right from the shoulder. (See Photo 8.17.)

PHOTO 8.15

PHOTO 8.16

Pivot in Tracks

This feed can be used in place of the jump turn, at a distance of 20–25 feet from second base. Beyond 25 feet, the jump turn is used to get more velocity on the throw. To get into position to make this type of feed, the second baseman fields the ground ball directly in front, with his left foot slightly ahead of his right foot. As he catches the ball, he pivots on the balls of his feet, turning his toes directly toward second base, and pivots at the hips so that the upper part of his body is facing second base squarely. He can go to his left knee when making a dart-type throw, right from the shoulder. This feed is eventually much faster than the jump turn, but it requires more practice to perfect the technique. (See Photo 8.18.)

PHOTO 8.17

PHOTO 8.18

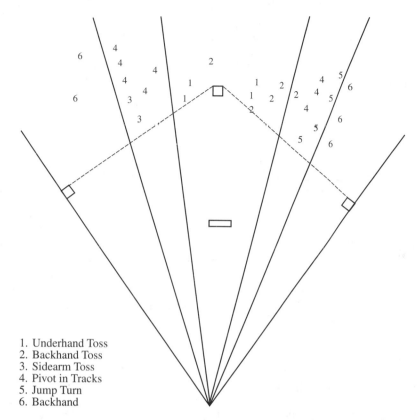

1. Underhand Toss
2. Backhand Toss
3. Sidearm Toss
4. Pivot in Tracks
5. Jump Turn
6. Backhand

FIGURE 8.2   Areas in the infield showing where feeds can be made by the shortstop and second baseman

Balls Hit to the Extreme Left of the Second Baseman

This play is the only time a player should turn his back on the person to whom he is throwing. As the second baseman fields the ball with his glove hand outstretched and his momentum going away from second base, he takes one more step with his right foot, which turns his back to home plate. He plants on his right foot and throws overhand to second base. The throw is aimed chest high to the shortstop, who should be positioned to the outfield side of second base. (See Figure 8.2.)

Drills for Improving Infield Drills

DRILL 8.1.   Infield Feed Drill

Purpose: To have infielders practice all feeds from the shortstop and second baseman and work on pivots.

Area Required: 20- or 30-foot square.

Equipment Needed: Gloves and ball. (See Figure 8.3.)

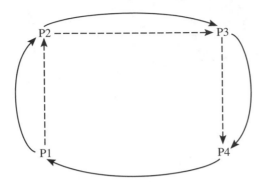

FIGURE 8.3   Infield feed drill

Procedure: Have two or three players at each place on the box. P1 rolls the ball to P2. P2 fields the ball and uses the underhand toss to P3. P3 catches the ball and makes a pivot as if he were a second baseman. He throws the ball to P4. P4 catches the ball and runs and replaces P1. All players rotate after catching or throwing the ball. After using the underhand toss, the infielders use the sidearm toss, the pivot-in-tracks toss, and the backhand play.

In this part of the drill, the direction is reversed. P1 rolls the ball to P4, who uses the backhand toss to P3. P3 catches the ball and makes a backhand toss to P2. P2 catches the ball and makes a backhand toss to P1. No pivots are made, and players stay in the same spot. Then they use the pivot-in-tracks toss and the jump turn.

DRILL 8.2.   Multiple Purpose Infield Drill

Purpose: To work on many areas of infield techniques.

Area Required: Infield. (See Figure 8.4.)

Equipment Needed: Balls and gloves.

Procedure: A coach positioned on the infield grass in front of second base rolls a ball to the shortstop, who feeds it to the second baseman. The second baseman pivots and throws to a *shagger,* who is positioned halfway between first and second base. The shagger returns the ball to the coach. The coach works on all feeds by the short-stop and then moves on to the second baseman, who works on all his feeds.

The coach at third base rolls the ball to the third baseman, who throws the ball across the diamond to first base. The first baseman throws the ball to home plate, where the catcher receives it and makes a throw to third base in an attempt to retire a runner trying to advance. The third baseman tags the runner and returns the ball to the coach. Players also work on bunt plays, slow rollers, balls to the left or right, and so on.

Note: All pivots and feeds should be used during the course of a practice session so the short-stop and second baseman become accustomed to each other. The feed will determine what type of pivot you will use, and you cannot turn the double play unless you get the lead man.

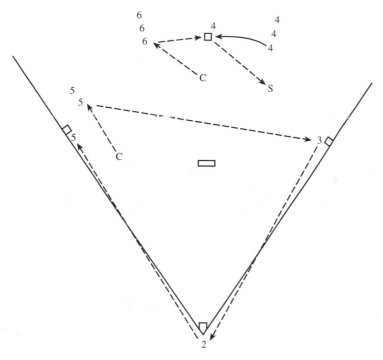

FIGURE 8.4

TIPS FOR THE DOUBLE PLAY

- This play must be smooth and coordinated to be effective.
- There are no set rules for making the pivot. Each fielder should make the pivot in the way best suited to his physical ability.
- All pivots can be improved upon by practice.
- Throws to the pivot man should be quick snap throws or dart throws.
- The second baseman throws to the outside corner of the base.
- The shortstop throws to the inside corner of the base.
- On plays close to the base, throw the ball underhand to the pivot man, with your body moving toward the base.
- Do not hide the ball. Take the ball out of your glove and move your glove hand completely out of the way.
- Do not be fancy with your toss—this takes away from the coordination of the play.
- Make all tosses letter high for easy handling.
- The pivot man's throw must be quick, with his body moving toward first base.
- Move your feet fast to avoid being taken out by the baserunner.
- If you are the pivot man, get to the base quickly.
- Shortstops and second baseman *must* warm up together before infield practice. This enables you to learn how the ball reacts when thrown from all angles by your partner.

9

OUTFIELD PLAY: MEANINGFUL
REPETITION OF DRILLS

Good defensive outfield play is one of the most important and most exciting phases in the game of baseball, yet it is rarely stressed and seldom taught properly. A confident outfielder wants the ball hit to him when the big out must be made. Proper defensive outfield play and knowledge of the fundamentals are important for all outfielders because they help them to become complete players. Being a complete player as an outfielder means, very simply, the ability to execute consistently while thinking and anticipating every aspect of defensive outfield play.

QUALIFICATIONS: THE BASIC FOUR

Let's look at the list of qualifications for outfielders, often referred to as the *basic four*.

1. Concentration: The ability to focus on the pitcher and the batter is an ideal starting point for outfielders. The key to good outfield play is the ability to react, and good reaction time is a direct result of total concentration. We have all seen a game in which the attention of one of the outfielders has wandered. He has not been tested throughout the contest, and suddenly he is called upon to make a defensive play. He reacts with a late jump, the ball gets by him, and perhaps the game is over, too. It is the responsibility of the coach to prepare the outfielders to be ready at all times, and it begins with the development of concentration.
2. Speed. The ability to get to the ball quickly is an asset. Outfielders must be able to cover their territory, especially if the field is not fenced in. Center field is usually the place for the fastest outfielder. He is responsible for cutting off the balls hit into the gaps.
3. Strong throwing arm. The ability to throw long and accurately is another important qualification for any good outfielder. Getting the ball back to the infield quickly and accurately keeps many a runner from advancing.

4. Knowledge of the situation. Throwing to the wrong base or trying a shoe-top catch at the wrong time has cost us all a game or two. An outfielder must be constantly aware of the following: What? Where? When? How? This means: What is the score? Where are the runners? He must know when and how to charge the ball and where to be so that he is prepared to make the primary and secondary throws. Consider the following list:

- Taking the proper set position.
- Getting good jumps on all batted balls.
- Charging a ground ball (rounding the ball for a throw).
- Backing up bases and all infielders on throws and batted balls.
- Playing angles on all hit balls—running a straight line to every hit ball—running good routes.
- Backing each other up.
- Going back on balls hit over your head from each outfield position.
- Getting behind fly balls to get into proper throwing position.
- Hitting the relay man.
- Hitting the cutoff man.
- Knowing the relay and cutoff man's responsibilities.
- Releasing the ball properly when throwing (6-12 rotation).
- Playing the fence.
- Compensating for sun and wind. Using glasses—how and why. Realizing that wind and sun can be different in various ball parks.
- Knowing the pitcher. Is he a fast-ball type, an off-speed type? What does he throw when behind? What does he throw when ahead? How good is his stuff on any given day?
- Playing the count.
- Knowing the hitter and situation—outs, score, men on base, and so on.
- Throwing to the proper base.
- Knowing when and when not to gamble on a catch.
- Assessing the speed of the ball and the speed of the runner to determine where to throw each batted ball.
- Knowing the infielder's ability to go back on the ball—to help you position yourself.
- Anticipating what you will do before every pitch if the ball is hit to you.
- Listening for the sound of the batted ball.
- Understanding that when the infield is up, the outfielders come up.
- Staying within yourself.
- When in doubt, keeping the double play in order and throwing to second base.

Good hitting outfielders who neglect developing their defensive abilities are really a questionable asset. If an outfielder gives up as many runs as he drives in, his worth to the team is clearly in question. By developing his skills through consistent execution of the fundamentals of baseball each day, the outfielder helps not only himself, but his team as well.

One more thing to remember is that skills, whether in a profession or in sports, cease to develop when we don't keep them fine tuned. Arms go bad when they are not kept in shape, fielding falls off without daily shagging and practice, and running speed diminishes when it is not exercised. The same holds true for defensive outfield play. Baseball is a game that keeps a player honest. If he neglects his skills, it will show on the field. It requires hard work to reach one's potential, and even more effort to stay there.

Numerous individuals associated with baseball on all levels are convinced of one very important secret to good defensive outfield play: an outfielder learns to play his position and get good jumps on the ball only one way—by shagging daily off the bat during live batting practice. An outfielder learns to read the swing of the hitter and the position of the pitch as he practices 15–20 minutes per day. On every pitch, the outfielder should pick up the direction of the ball off the bat, moving quickly four or five steps in that direction whether or not contact has been made.

Constant repetition of this fundamental outfield drill improves an outfielder's defensive ability. When the ball is hit, the outfielders play it just as though it were in a game. Fungo hitting to outfielders is good for conditioning, loosening up, working on individual skills, and developing the hands, but the only place an outfielder learns to go after the ball is in live batting practice, where many balls are hit and he must react to them.

As coaches and instructors, we have seen dramatic improvement in the poorest of outfielders over the course of a season. Of course, the key is daily shagging, dedication, execution, and hard work. If an infielder can work at his defensive abilities every day prior to ball games, so can an outfielder.

Remember: reading the position of the pitch, the arc of the swing, the sound of the ball hitting the bat, and the strength of the swing are all part of learning to play the outfield. If they concentrate on it, corner fielders can become so sharp reading a pitch that they will be able to read inside and outside pitches as well as the center fielders do.

GENERAL OUTFIELD FUNDAMENTALS

Stance

An outfielder should *come set* before every pitch in a game, anticipating that each pitched ball may be hit to him. *Coming set* means his going from a stand-up position prior to the pitch, taking a step or two forward to a bent-knee position with his weight on the balls of his feet and his hands either resting lightly on his knees or hanging loosely in front of his body, and thus being ready to move in any direction as the pitch is made. Some outfielders like to have body movement in the set position because a body in motion tends to remain in motion, while a motionless body tends to stay motionless. It is difficult to get a motionless body moving.

Remember: after each pitch, the outfielder can straighten up if the pitch is taken by the batter. He then steps back and begins again as the pitcher prepares to deliver the next pitch. He follows the flight of the pitch, reading the swing and the bat angle while listening for sound as contact is made. Playing each pitch and swing with the utmost concentration cannot be overemphasized.

Breaking on Balls

All outfielders break on balls left and right by using the crossover step or short jab step. When a ball is hit directly over the head of the center fielder, he should drop the foot on his glove side and cross over with his opposite leg. This puts the glove in a better reaching position for the running over-the-shoulder catch. An outfielder always looks back over the shoulder on the side from which he broke. Balls hit over the center fielder's head usually have a 6-12 rotation and no hook or slice. Therefore, a good center fielder can see the ball as it is hit, break for it, and take one look during the run as he comes under the ball, either standing and waiting for it or reaching out at the last second if a running catch is in order. He runs with his knees and feet going in the same flight path as the ball. He does not side-step, and he keeps his upper body squared away.

Balls hit over the right and left fielder's heads normally have rotation, which causes the ball to move to the foul line regardless of whether it is hit by a left- or right-handed hitter. The right and left fielders should always open toward the foul line on balls hit directly over their heads. During the flight of the ball, they must take two or three looks before the catch to stay in the flight path of the ball. If the fielder is in a poor pattern for a fly ball, he adjusts by turning in toward the infield; then he continues. He does not take his eyes off the ball. On line drives, he always turns in toward the infield; on high fly balls, he can turn his back and make a full turn.

The outfield corners must get to the foul line as quickly as possible on balls hit down the line, and they must attempt to turn doubles into possible outs. When fielding a ball hit down the line, right-handed right fielders and left-handed left fielders can turn their backs to the infield in preparing for the throw to second base. Center fielders going to glove side step over the ball and throw back to the infield.

Chinked balls off the end of the bat, which look as though they are hit but are not, can be given the best effort and battle only by an outfielder. In many cases, fast-moving infielders can make these plays and help the outfielders. Bloop hits over the infield belong

PHOTO 9.1

first to the outfielder, who should make every catch he can, and second to the infielder, who makes the catch only when he sees that it is impossible for the outfielder to do so. It is the infielder's responsibility to avoid collisions.

Thinking Ahead

Catching a ball is fun. Knowing what to do with it after catching it is business. Good outfielders always know what to do with the ball if it is hit to them before the pitcher releases it. Having an idea on a pitch is what keeps outfielders mentally in the game. They must know the hitter's and the runners' abilities at all times. THINK AHEAD.

Backup Responsibilities

On base hits to the outfield, each outfielder must back up his teammates. Center fielder backs up left and right, and the right and left fielders back up the center fielder, depending on where the ball is hit. The outfield backs up the infield on balls hit to them, just as though the infielders were going to miss the ball. Outfielders must be alert and moving to back up all throws from the catcher and all pickoff attempts by the pitchers. Knowing the pickoff signs is important; this knowledge helps develop and maintain a positive mental focus. (See Figure 9.1.)

Communication

Communication between the outfielders is essential. An outfielder must never drift on a fly ball because drifting makes it difficult for him to determine which outfielder will make the catch. A good rule to follow on fly balls is that all outfielders must move toward the ball; the call is made by the outfielder in the best fielding position as the ball starts downward. When a player calls for the ball, he should yell "I got it" at least twice, maybe even three times. Those around him should respond "Take it, Don" at least three times. Two important points must be made here: First, a system must be used and adhered to; second, one fielder should never presume to make a call for another fielder.

After the ball is called for, the other outfielders should not approach the caller's area, because the sound of footsteps could cause him to shy away from the ball. When two outfielders can make the catch and there is a runner on base tagging up, the fielder in the best throwing position should make the catch; in other situations the fielder with the stronger arm should make it. Communication is important, as you can see.

Collisions can be minimized if players follow these rules: When the center fielder and left fielder converge on a fly ball, the center fielder catches the ball low and the left fielder high. In right center field, the center fielder again catches low and the right fielder high. This keeps the outfielders off a collision course. On extra-base hits, the nonfielding outfielder gives the fielding outfielder only a verbal command: "Hit the relay man."

Bloopers over the Infield

All pop-ups over the infield belong to the outfielders. An infielder makes the catch only when an outfielder cannot reach the ball. Therefore it is important for the outfielders and

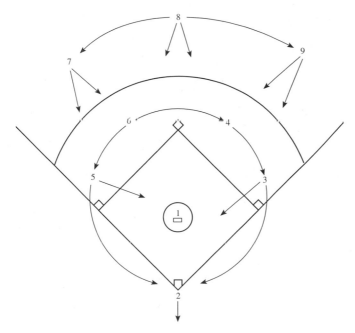

FIGURE 9.1 Fly ball and pop-up priorities. Center fielder (8) has priority over left fielder (7) and right fielder (9) and all infielders (5), (6), (4), and (3). Left fielder (7) and right fielder (9) have priority over all infielders (5), (6), (4), and (3). Shortstop (6) has priority over all other infielders (5), (4), and (3). Shortstop (6) and second baseman (4) have priority over third baseman (5) and first baseman (3). Third baseman (5) and first baseman (3) have priority over catcher (2) and pitcher (1). Catcher (2) takes anything that the third baseman (5) and first baseman (3) cannot reach. Pitcher (1) is the last man on the totem pole. He takes anything no one can reach.

infielders to know one another's speed, range, and ability to go back on pop-ups. Following are three basic ways for an outfielder to catch this type of batted ball:

1. Diving forward with glove arm extended and landing on his stomach. This is dangerous because of the force the body puts on the arm and shoulder; occasionally shoulders are separated and dislocated. When diving to his right or left on balls hit in gaps or down the line, as soon as the catch is made, he raises his hand and takes the force of the fall on his chest. This helps to prevent injury.

2. Catch and roll. This is very difficult, but some coaches like it. The play is made by extending the glove hand, catching the ball, and somersaulting, taking the blow with the ground on the back.

3. Bent-leg slide. This is the most popular and the least dangerous. The fielder slides just as though he were using a bent-leg slide into a base. The glove is placed over the bent leg and calf. Remember the game situation before diving for line drive balls that will roll a long way if missed.

KNOWLEDGE OF OPPONENTS

Outfielders and Pitchers Should Know Their Opponents

It is important that all outfielders know all they can about pitchers' abilities, their strong suits, and what is working at the time. If a pitcher is throwing a lot of slow stuff and junk, he plays most hitters to pull; for hard stuff, he plays more straightaway. A good percentage for positioning the outfield is to play the count with the pitcher's ability. A good outfielder knows all of the hitters on the opposing team and where they hit the ball most often, and he gives consideration to how well or poorly the pitcher is throwing that particular day. Following is a chart that show how an outfielder may move on various counts to the hitter.

Count	Steps to Pull Side		Steps to Nonpull Side	
0-0				
1-1				
2-2				
1-0	3 to 4	(Hitter looking for pitch)		
2-0	5 to 6	(Hitter looking for pitch)		
3-0	8 to 10	(Hitter looking for pitch)		
3-1	5 to 6	(Hitter looking for pitch)		
3-2	3 to 4	(Hitter looking for pitch)		
2-1	2	(Hitter looking for pitch)		
0-1			2	(protecting plate)
1-2			3	(protecting plate)
0-2			4	(protecting plate)

Note: All outfielders must move. Otherwise a gap may cause a weakness in the defense.

CATCHING, THROWING, AND FIELDING SKILLS

Playing the Fences

The tendency many outfielders have is to play too close to the fence. If a ballpark has short fences, the outfielders should close the gap between themselves and the infielders. The distance is based on the outfielder's ability to go back on balls. In going for a ball hit to the fence, the outfielder goes to the fence as quickly as possible, places his throwing hand on the fence, and then goes along the fence to make the catch. For balls that do not quite reach the fence, he moves toward the infield a step or two to make the catch. In both examples, he must get to the fence first.

When jumping near a fence to catch a fly ball, the outfielder jumps with his body sideways and his throwing hand on fence, never with his rear end against the fence. Before games, outfielders should always check the fences for bounce by throwing a ball against them. Different fences (concrete, wood, ivy, screen, foam rubber, and so on) produce different bounces. A warning track gives the outfielder two to three steps' notice. Each outfielder should remind the others to back one another up on batted balls that are sure to hit a fence, and not to get too close to the fence to field the bounce.

Playing the Sun Field

When using sunglasses, an outfielder normally flips the lens down as the ball approaches the sun. He does not wait until the ball gets into the sun or until it is on its downward flight. This is too late. Good glasses reduce the sun to a small spot with little glare around it. Thus the outfielder can follow the ball easily to make the catch. Today there are sunglasses that outfielders can wear all the time.

On occasion the outfielder can angle his body away from the sun, which helps in the catch. Some outfielders like to use their glove as a sun shield, blocking the sun with the glove during the entire flight of the ball. A good rule of thumb: Flip glasses down before the ball reaches the highest point of flight and before getting into the sun. Never flip the glasses down until the flight of the ball has been zeroed in.

Two-Hand Catches

Having the throwing hand around the glove at all times during the catch is a very good practice. Using two hands, the fielder is mechanically correct for plays that require a throw after the catch. Catching with two hands helps the outfielder learn to finger the ball early; he does not get into the bad habit of catching one-handed and bringing the glove hand and ball to the throwing hand. Having the throwing hand around the glove reduces the time needed to gain control of the ball and to get a good grip on it when throwing.

Getting a Proper Angle on Batted Balls

A very difficult fundamental for outfielders in the approach to fly and ground balls hit up the alleys is to play the ball in a straight line so that they intersect it either in the air or on the ground, running after it in a straight line. Rounding balls allows fly balls to fall in for extra base hits and ground balls to go for extra base hits instead of possible outs.

When playing proper angles on line drives to the right and left, outfielders must stare the ball down. Going to the right or left while keeping his eyes on the ball does not slow an outfielder down. Good right and left fielders go to the foul lines and turn possible hits into outs.

Throwing after Fly Ball Catch

The outfielder has two very important adjustments to make when a runner is on base and is tagging to advance on a fly ball:

1. He must round the ball to be in a direct line with the base to which he will throw.
2. He must take throwing steps before making the catch. He does this by setting up three to four steps behind the ball, then charging the ball, taking throwing steps as he fields the ball in front of his body above the letters. He makes the catch quickly, with his throwing hand around his glove, enabling him to finger the ball for a good proper grip. A strong crow hop allows his arm to reach back to complete the throw.

Playing Line Drives

Line drives are difficult and tough to read when they are hit directly at the outfielder. He must watch the line drive all the way, using a freeze or drop step until he is certain where the ball is going. He always keeps his eyes on the ball. On occasion, every outfielder gets a ball coming like a knuckle ball. It hops, drops, and moves. The fielder must be loose and ready to give it battle by hanging with it throughout its flight. A helpful coaching tip: Line drives hit at the fielder and below the bill of his baseball cap are played in front of him; line drives above the bill of the cap require that the outfielder go back on the ball.

No Man's Land

Good outfielders avoid getting into what is frequently called *No Man's Land.* This happens when an outfielder reacts slowly on a line drive hit into his area. Because of a late jump, he allows himself to be handcuffed by the ball, and in most cases the ball gets by him. To avoid this problem, an outfielder must use quick judgment as to whether he *can* make the catch and whether he *should* make the catch. Gambling on line drives should occur only if the game is on the line. Diving for a line drive in front of him is never a good idea in early innings. Diving for pop-ups that do not roll far away from the fielder is more acceptable. Quick judgment is attained in practice, shagging off the bat daily.

Fielding Ground Balls

Outfielders field ground balls as close to the infield as possible, or they charge them; they never let the ball play them. With no one on base, it is permissible to go down on one knee to field the ball. This position helps to block the ball with the body if the fielder misses the ball. The outfielder must get the ball back to the infield quickly. With men on base necessitating a throw, he fields the ball on the glove side with the foot on that side forward, catching the ball in front of that foot or off to the side, perhaps 6–12 inches. After fielding the ball, he brings his opposite leg forward, then does a crow hop and throws. The crow hop can be on both feet, like an infielder's, or on the leg opposite the glove hand after it comes forward.

An important point for an outfielder when fielding ground balls that require a throw is to round the ball, getting into position so that his momentum is directly toward the base to which he is throwing. Three basic speeds are used by the outfielder when charging a ground ball to make a throw:

1. Fast. The initial move to the ball is fast.
2. Gather. This speed is used just before fielding. The body is slowed to a controlled fielding position, which allows the outfielder to gather himself (to get himself under control).
3. Fast again. Following the fielding of the ball from the position, the throwing steps to release are fast again. The outfielder gets his throwing hand around the glove as quickly as possible to gain control of the ball for the throw.

Coaching cue: Fast to ball, then field, step, crow hop, throw.

Throwing

The outfielder's throw is overhand and gripped across the seams. The thrown ball must have direct backspin or 6-12 rotation for the following reasons:

1. The ball will stay up longer and on a straight line.
2. When the ball hits the ground, the backspin causes a biting effect, giving a good bounce to the fielder receiving the ball. Side spin or three-quarter spin causes the ball to run away from the fielder receiving the ball.

An outfielder never throws behind a runner unless there is no play on the lead runner. He thinks ahead so that when the ball is hit to him, he has an idea of where to go with the throw. The depth that is played, the speed of the runners, the speed of the hit ball, and the arm strength of the player making the defensive play are all factors that go into determining immediately where the throw is going. When in doubt, the outfielder goes to second base.

Hitting the Relay Man

One of the outfielder's most difficult throws and most important skills is hitting the relay man. The *relay man* is the second baseman or the shortstop who goes out to take a relay throw from the outfielders on extra base hits. With rare exceptions, the outfielder should not be confused as to what he will do with the ball when he fields it. He has only one play: *hit the relay man.*

The depth of the relay man is determined by the size of the ballpark, the strength of the outfielder's arm, and the relay man's own arm strength. A short fence and a strong-armed outfielder do not require that the relay man come out deep.

In any case, the outfielder gives the relay man a line drive throw, which the relay man can field over his glove shoulder while on the move toward the infield. This type of throw lets the relay man get moving toward the infield and allows him to have more zip on his throw. The outfielder should throw to the glove side of the relay man because the latter can adjust to his glove side more easily than he could if the throw were on the throwing side.

The trailer is 20–25 feet behind the relay man and is directing the play. The trailer fields all overthrows and low throws. The relay man pulls away from these poor throws to allow the trailer to get them. Note: It is better to overthrow the relay man than to underthrow him. The trailer can field an overthrow.

Hitting the Cutoff Man

Outfielders should know their responsibilities and those of their cutoff man. Let's look at various fielders as the cutoff man:

First Baseman

The first baseman sets up about mound depth for throws from right field to home plate. Throws should be letter high. On throws from center field, the first baseman sets up 2–3 feet from the pitcher's rubber on the home plate side. This keeps the mound in front of him so that if he cuts the ball off, he has a better feel for the mound and can use the added height to his advantage. In addition, if a throw from center field is low, the first baseman can see whether it is going to hit the mound and go off to the first- or third-base line. The first baseman knows to cut this type of throw.

By playing on the mound, the first baseman gives the center fielder a better look at the mound for his throw over it. Some first basemen play on the second-base side of the mound. This is permissible, but the deeper the cutoff man can play on the throw without causing a short hop to the running infielder, the better, for the following reasons:

1. The outfielder must stretch his throw to hit the cutoff man in the chest.
2. By being deeper, the cutoff man has a better glimpse of the runner.
3. The infielder taking the throw can wait longer to make the call to "cut."
4. The cutoff man's judgment as to whether he has a chance at the runner is greatly improved because he is closer to the bag. This allows him to prepare mentally to cut or let the ball go through.
5. The cutoff man can creep toward the ball so that his throwing steps are taken before the cut, giving him some zip on his throw.

The Third Baseman on Throws from Left Field

The third baseman lines up about mound height for a throw to home. The shortstop lines up about mound height for throw from center field to third base and right field to third base. Remember: the cutoff men must adjust to the outfielder's arm strength.

Outfielders' Toughest Plays

1. Charging a ground ball to throw a runner out.
2. Setting up behind a fly ball to throw a runner out.
3. Hitting the relay man with a perfect throw.
4. Hitting the cutoff man with a letter-high throw.
5. Going back on balls.
6. Fielding a chinker off the end of the bat after a big swing.
7. Playing angles to the ball in straight lines.
8. Getting to foul lines quickly and turning doubles into outs.
9. Cutting balls off in the gaps.

Drills for Improving Outfield Skills

DRILL 9.1.   Ground Ball Approach

Purpose: To work on the approach to ground balls. To instruct in the five essentials for good fielding.

Area Required: Indoor or outdoor area for ground balls.

Equipment Needed: Fungo and baseballs or a machine that throws baseballs.

Procedure: Balls are hit on the ground to outfielders so that they can:

1. Charge or come hard.
2. Run low.
3. Gather themselves or break down under control to get the big hop.
4. Explode into the ball at the big hop.
5. Field the ball out in front and on the left side (right-handed fielder) and on the right side (left-handed fielder).

DRILL 9.2.   Fielding Response Drill

Purpose: To develop response speed and proper footwork.

Area Required: Indoor or outdoor area for ground balls.

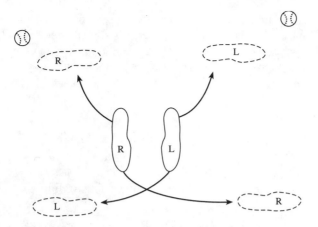

FIGURE 9.2

> **Equipment Needed:** Fungo and baseballs.
>
> **Procedure:** Hit balls to the right and left and directly at the outfielders: line drives, long fly balls, and others. The footwork is to be observed and corrected. (See Figures 9.2 and 9.3.)

DRILL 9.3. Charge, Scoop and Throw, or Do or Die

Purpose: To learn the proper method of charging the ball.

Area Required: Indoor or outdoor space for ground balls.

Equipment Needed: Fungo and baseballs.

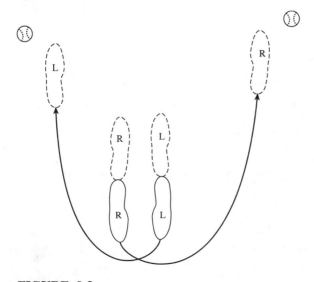

FIGURE 9.3

Procedure: Balls are hit directly at the outfielders, who must make a throw to cut down a runner. The game is on the line. An outfielder starts for the ball on a dead sprint, approaches the ball, gets under control, fields the ball one-handed on the outside of his glove leg, and throws to the plate. The coach observes the head in this drill. It should be kept up, which allows the arm to do most of the work and keeps the throw low.

DRILL 9.4   Tag Up and Throw

Purpose: To teach proper footwork on a tag-up fly ball.

Area Required: Indoor or outdoor space.

Equipment Needed: Fungo, baseballs, possible machine for throwing.

Procedure: The ball is thrown or batted. The outfielder attempts to stand a step behind the ball so that if he throws with his right hand, he will be stepping forward with his right foot as he catches the ball. This provides the momentum and arm-leg coordination needed to make the throw strong and accurate without wasting time on additional steps.

DRILL 9.5.   Short Fly Balls

Purpose: To teach outfielders to recognize which short fly balls they can catch and which they cannot.

Area Required: Indoor or outdoor space for short fly balls.

Equipment Needed: Fungo and baseballs.

Procedure: The outfield starts running before the ball is hit or thrown. The drill allows the players to recognize their own abilities as to which balls they can get to and which ones they cannot.

DRILL 9.6.   Playing the Ball in the Sun

Purpose: To develop the ability to play the ball in the sun.

Area Required: Outdoors on a *sunny day.*

Equipment Needed: Fungo and baseballs.

Procedure: Position the outfielders and hit fungos so that all balls for them will be directly in the sun. The outfielder starts running before the ball is hit or thrown toward him. The outfielder tries to catch the ball on the fly, and if he cannot, he tries to keep the ball from getting past him. The basics that were mentioned earlier should be emphasized.

DRILL 9.7.   Finding the Fence

Purpose: To develop the skill of getting to the fence and catching the ball.

Area Required: Indoor or outdoor space near a fence or wall.

Equipment Needed: Fungo and baseballs.

Procedure: A great deal of work can be accomplished indoors with this drill because walls are all around and can be used as fences. Make sure that the wall is padded in some way, because you are trying to build confidence in the outfielders' ability to find the fence. Start hitting fungos close to the wall or fence and gradually move farther away. Outfielders should develop the habit of feeling for the fence. Before you throw the ball, give the outfielder time to find the fence. Decrease the amount of time as his ability improves, and work to a point at which he is breaking to the wall at the same time the ball is being hit or tossed to the fence. In the final step of the drill, the outfielder has to break to the fence without looking at the ball, judging where the ball will land and getting to the fence at that spot.

DRILL 9.8.   Overhead Fly Ball Drill

Purpose: To teach outfielders to play the ball overhead and deep.

Area Required: Infield, right field, left field.

Equipment Needed: Two fungos and six baseballs for each side.

Procedure: Split outfielders between left and right fields. Place fungo hitters in third- and first-base fungo circles and a relay player in each coaching box. Move outfielders out about 150 feet from a fungo hitter. Have the hitter loft continuous fly balls deep to alternating players. After catching the ball, they throw it to the relay man on their side. Switch outfield groups to give all players experience with sun and wind changes.

DRILL 9.9.   Working the Cutoff Man

Purpose: To teach outfielders how to hit the cutoff man.

Area Required: Outfield area to provide a throwing distance of 110–130 feet.

Equipment Needed: A screen with a towel.

Procedure: A large protective screen takes the place of the cutoff man, and a towel is tied to the screen to indicate the specific target. Outfielders are positioned 110–130 feet from the screen. The coach hits a ground ball so that the outfielder charges it and uses the correct footwork and throwing techniques to make a good throw at the towel or the screen. This can also be made into a competition drill if the group is divided into two teams and points are awarded for hitting the screen or towel. Points are subtracted for bad footwork and for missing the screen entirely.

DRILL 9.10.   Outfielder Awareness Drill

Purpose: To help outfielders learn not to shy away from each other in close quarters and to teach them how to make the proper priority call.

Area Required: Either indoor or outdoor space.

Equipment Needed: Baseballs.

Procedure: The coach throws the ball between two converging outfielders running at a 45-degree angle on a ball in the gap. One outfielder should take the proper angle and make the proper priority call at the appropriate time.

DRILL 9.11.   Throwing-Machine Station

Purpose: To teach shagging in a game situation. To improve footwork and strides in covering ground and to condition and work on forehand and backhand catching.

Equipment Needed: Machine, feeder, and bucket with baseballs.

Procedure: Lock in the machine to throw to the same spot. Players start from the first of six stations. The ball goes up and players work on getting to it, catching it with two hands, and throwing over the shoulder. Players rotate to all stations (some require different approach angles and catching positions).

For the second part of this drill, the machine is set for line drives. The players are now divided into two groups. One group runs hard left to catch line drives, while the other runs hard right. After the catch, the fielder goes to the back of the other group. One player catches at a time, and the machine is not fed until the player has cleared the area.

For the third part of this drill, the machine is set for a routine fly ball. The player sets up behind the ball and works on approaching the ball to throw out a runner who is tagging up. The player must catch the ball with two hands and crow hop quickly.

DRILL 9.12.   Three-Ball Drill

Purpose: To condition and to teach the use of a glove for both forehand and backhand catches.

Area Required: Left- or right-field line.

Equipment Needed: One dozen baseballs.

Procedure: The outfielder begins a hard run from either the right- or left-field line. The coach positions himself 30–35 yards away from the player running and about one-third of the distance from center field. The coach's first throw is a line drive that is catchable but high. The coach then moves about 10 yards toward center field and throws a low line drive. The coach's final throw is a lob throw over his head as the outfielder runs away from the coach. As ball is caught, the outfielder keeps running and flips the ball back with the throwing hand to the retriever. If there is a poor throw or overthrow, the retriever will pick up the ball. After all reach one side, go the other way. This works on both forehand and backhand and keeps players running as well. The coach can also correct poor running habits and help improve the stride distance of the players.

10

TEAM DEFENSE: PHILOSOPHY AND DRILLS

Team defense starts with the word *attitude*. Nobody will ever catch the ball if he doesn't want to. To be successful, the whole team must want to play defense. Human beings play the game of baseball, so there are always going to be errors of commission and omission, but the good teams keep them to a limited number. Confidence, as displayed by the entire team in aggressively attacking the ball on defense, is also a positive factor in developing a defensive attitude. Team defense is the direct outgrowth of every player's involvment in playing a ball.

For a team to be an effective unit on the field, the coach must develop a team plan. It is important for him to use drills that have a purpose and help him teach the proper way to handle various situations. Coaches should school their players to recognize game situations and react to them. No situation should be taken for granted, because one player never knows how an opposing player is going to react. A coach does not want the opposing team to capitalize on a mistake because his team was not ready to react to it.

Communication and movement are vital to good team defense. Every player should be moving on a batted or thrown ball and should be ready to call out to help a teammate.

Let's look at a list of basics for team defense before we get into situations and drills.

THE BASICS OF TEAM DEFENSE

Each player should:

- Always anticipate and want the ball hit to him.
- Always be ready to field his position.
- Know what he will do with the ball before it is hit.

- Be aggressive in playing the ball, not letting it play him.
- Know the playing field: fence, grass infield, skin infield, ground rules, and so on.
- Know who should be covering a base in a particular situation. Players should use signs or oral communication.
- Watch the ball and catch it first. A play has never been completed without the ball first being caught.
- Know the pitcher's ability and repertoire of pitches.
- Know and study the opponents, both at bat and in the field.
- Know the wind and sun conditions on the field. Players must check for changes every inning.
- Know his fly ball and pop fly priorities.
- Know the basics for his position and add them to this list.

DEFENSIVE CUTOFF AND RELAY PRINCIPLES

1. Whenever possible, all bases at which a play could occur should be covered.
2. The cutoff man must think quickly and anticipate the play. He must know beforehand which runner is the most important to put out. The coach must alert his team before the pitch as to what should be done. When the game is on the line, the coach must take the responsibility and make the decision. The entire team should be well drilled in cutoff and relay positioning.
3. Communication is important, not only between the cutoff man and the player covering the base, but especially among outfielders on balls hit between them and over their heads.
4. Infielders should not interfere with the baserunners but should position themselves inside the base. This tends to make the runner take a wider turn. The infielders should watch the runner touch the base. Many outs are recorded because of this heads-up procedure.
5. Outfielders should practice strong, low throws to all bases and to cutoff men.
6. Following are some common terms in cutoffs and relays:
   Cut: Cut this throw and hold the ball.
   Relay: Cut the ball and relay to the next base.
   Say nothing: Let the throw go through.

THE TANDEM OR PIGGYBACK RELAY

This relay is used by the shortstop and second baseman on a batted ball that is a sure double or a possible triple. On a batted ball to left field, left center field, or center field, the shortstop is the lead man. On a batted ball to right center field or right field, the second baseman is the lead man. The coach can change this procedure and let the player with the stronger arm always be the lead man.

The lead man sprints into the outfield in the direction of the batted ball. His right hand is raised straight above his head, and his glove hand is outstretched, parallel to the ground. When the outfielder retrieves the ball, he turns, finds the relay man, and then throws the ball to his glove side. As the ball is coming toward him, the relay man turns toward his glove side and starts drifting back toward the infield. As he catches the ball, his momentum should be in the direction to which he wants to throw. He gets rid of the ball as quickly as possible.

The back man positions himself 15–20 feet behind the lead man. The back man lines up the lead man and tells him where to throw the ball. He also backs up the lead man in case of an errant throw by the outfielder. If the throw is over the lead man's head or if he has to jump to catch it, he lets it go. The back man should be in position to catch the ball on a fly or on one bounce, after which he makes the throw to the infield. If the throw to the lead man is a short hop or an in-between hop, he steps out of the way and lets the ball go to the back man, who makes the throw to the infield.

SAMPLE TEAM DEFENSIVE SITUATIONS

This section shows sample game situations, with emphasis on two major defensive areas: cutoffs and relays, and defensive assignments in bunt situations. Team defense is most apparent and involved in these two areas. Regardless of the method used, the main emphasis is on doing it right. The defense is set up to get the lead runner, and all drills and practices are designed to meet this task.

We begin with a typical game situation, such as a single to left field with no runners on base. We then list each player and explain each of his defensive assignments in relation to the rest of the team. To help you visualize each situation further, a fully illustrated diagram is provided.

CUTOFF AND RELAYS

Situation #1A

Single to Left Field with No One on Base

Pitcher (1)	Take a position halfway between mound and second base (nose for ball).
Catcher (2)	Remain at home or move toward first base
First Baseman (3)	Observe the runner tagging the base when he makes his turn and covers the base.
Second Baseman (4)	Back up the shortstop at second base.
Third Baseman (5)	Observe activity; protect third-base area; be ready in case of poor throw.
Shortstop (6)	Take throw from left fielder at second base.
Left Fielder (7)	Throw strong, low throw to second base.
Center Fielder (8)	Back up left fielder.
Right Fielder (9)	Advance toward first-base area, lining up with throw from left fielder, in case of poor throw.

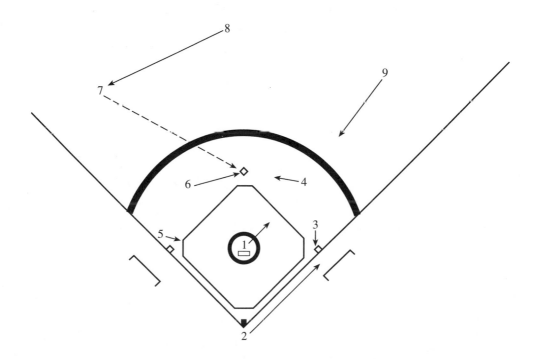

CUTOFF AND RELAYS

Situation #1B

Single to Left Field with No One on Base

Note: The difference between 2 and 3 is that the shortstop goes out to the cutoff position. All other actions by players are basically the same.

Observe movement of second baseman (4) and first baseman (3).

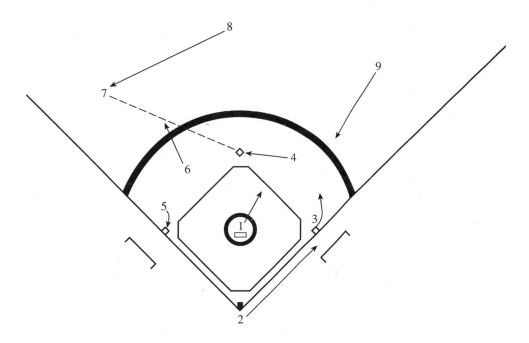

Situation #2

Single to Left Field with Man on First Base

Player:

1. Move to back up third base.

2. Remain at home plate to protect against a runner scoring.

3. Cover first base.

4. Cover second base.

5. Cover third base.

6. Become the cutoff man on the throw from the left fielder to third base.

7. Make a low, strong throw through cutoff man to third base.

8. Move to back up left fielder.

9. Move toward the infield to assist if necessary.

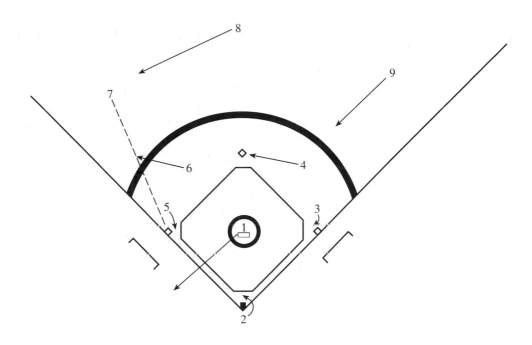

Situation #3

Single to Left Field with Runner on Second Base or Runners on First and Third Bases

Player:

1. Move halfway between second and home and observe the play as it develops.

2. Remain at home plate for possible play.

3. Cover first base and observe play development.

4. Cover second base and observe play development.

5. Assume the role of cutoff man between left fielder and home.

6. Cover third base and observe play development.

7. Charge the ball while under control and make strong, low throw through cutoff man to home plate.

8. Back up left fielder and offer communication as to play development.

9. Move toward second base area.

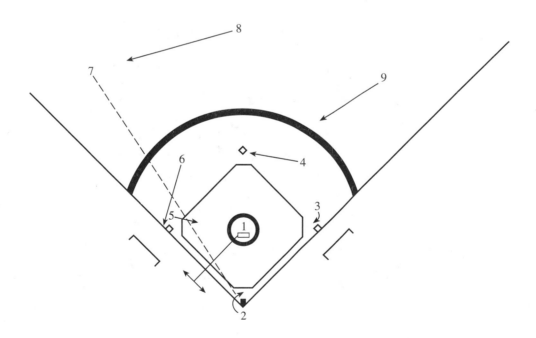

Situation #4

Single to Left Field between Third and Short with Runners on Second Base or on Second and Third Bases

Player:

1. Back up home plate.

2. Cover home plate.

3. Stay near first base.

4. Cover second base.

5. Cutoff man to home plate.

6. Cover third.

7. Make strong, low throw to home plate.

8. Move to back up left fielder.

9. Come in to assist and possibly cover first base, if necessary.

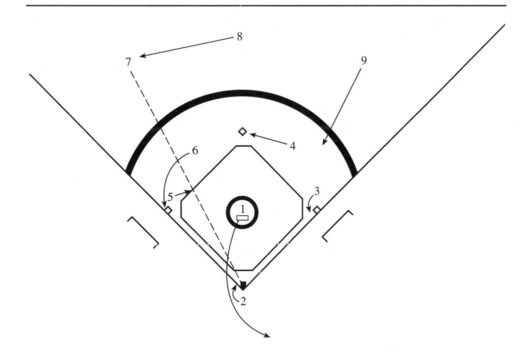

Situation #5

Double, Possible Triple, to Left Center Field with Runners on Third and Second Bases, on Both Third and Second Bases, or No One on Base

Player:

1. Be halfway between third and home; watch play develop.

2. Remain at home.

3. Follow or trail the batter (runner) to second base; cover the bag in case a play develops if runner rounds base too far.

4. Become the second man or backup man in the double relay; trail the shortstop by approximately 30 feet while in line with third base.*

5. Cover third base; position yourself on left side of base.

6. Be the main or premier relay man; go out to left field to get throw from outfielder. First or lead man in double relay.

7. Make low, hard throw to shortstop; do not try to throw to third base.

8. Back up left fielder or make throw as above if he gets to ball first.

9. Come in to back up second base.

*Double relay is used for two purposes:
   a. To back the first relay man in case of a bad throw.
   b. To tell the first relay man what to do when he receives the ball from the outfielder. This is sometimes referred to as a "piggyback relay."

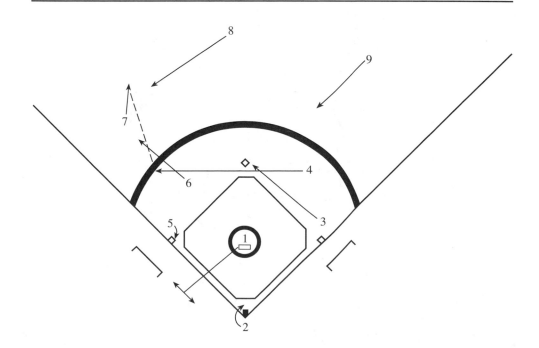

Situation #6

Double, Possible Triple, to Left Center Field with Runners on First Base, on First and Second Bases, or Perhaps Loaded Bases

Player:

1. Be prepared to watch play develop; go halfway between third and home and then back up the base where the play develops.

2. Stay at home plate.

3. Trail runner to second base and then be the cutoff man from the double relay group.

4. Be the second man of the double relay, about 30 feet behind the shortstop, in line with throw from outfield to either third or home. Alert shortstop as to possible play.

5. Cover third base; stand on left side of base.

6. Go to get first throw from left fielder; relay man **1**.

7. Make strong throw to shortstop.

8. Back up left fielder.

9. Move toward infield to assist if necessary.

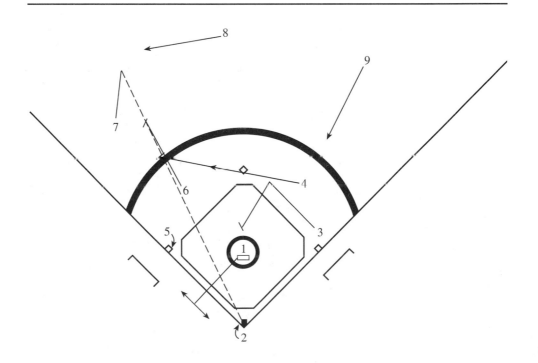

Situation #7

Double, Perhaps Triple, Down Left-Field Foul Line with Man on First Base

Player:

1. Watch play develop, halfway between home and third.

2. Remain to cover home plate.

3. Follow runner toward second base and become cutoff man if needed.

4. Be the second part of the double relay (trailer), behind the shortstop.

5. Cover third base.

6. Relay man **1**.

7. Make strong throw to shortstop.

8. Back up the left fielder.

9. Cover toward infield (right side).

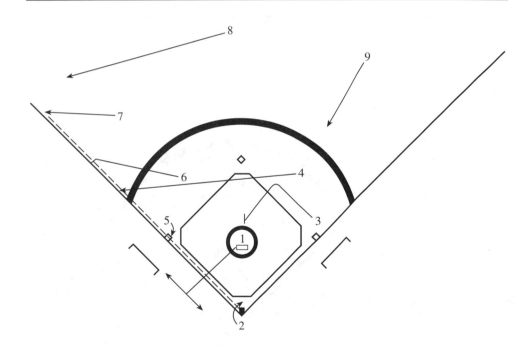

Situation #8

Single to Center Field with No Runners on Base

Player:

1. Observe play and move to position half-way between mound and second base.

2. Remain at home plate.

3. Make sure runner tags first base when making the turn, remain at first to protect in case of a rundown, and so on.

4. Watch throw from center and back up throw to shortstop covering second.

5. Remain at third.

6. Cover center fielder's throw to second base.

7. Round behind center fielder and communicate with him.

8. Make strong, low throw to second base.

9. Do same as left fielder (7).

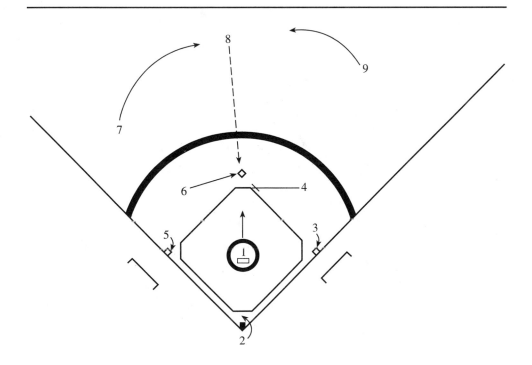

Situation #9

Single to Center Field with Runner on First Base

Player:

1. Move to back up third base.

2. Remain at home plate.

3. Cover first base.

4. Cover second base.

5. Remain at third; cover base.

6. Be the cutoff man between center fielder and third base.

7. Move toward third base in foul ground.

8. Make strong, hard, low throw to third base.

9. Back up center fielder.

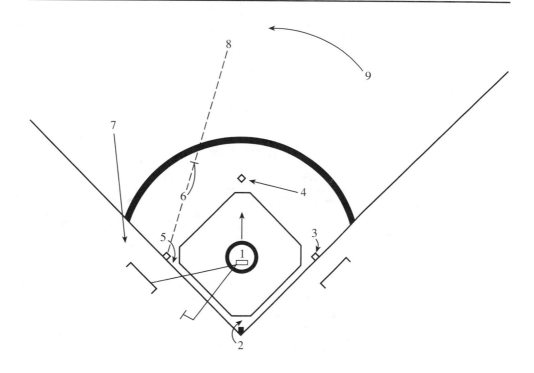

Situation #10

Single to Center Field with Runner on Second Base or Runners on Second and Third Bases

Player:

1. Move to back up home plate.

2. Protect home plate.

3. Move to cutoff position.

4. Attempt to field ball and move to assist by verbal communication.

5. Remain at third for possible play.

6. Attempt to field ball; then cover second base.

7. Back up center fielder: communication!

8. Make strong, low throw to plate, over the cutoff man's head but within fielding area.

9. Back up center fielder: communication!

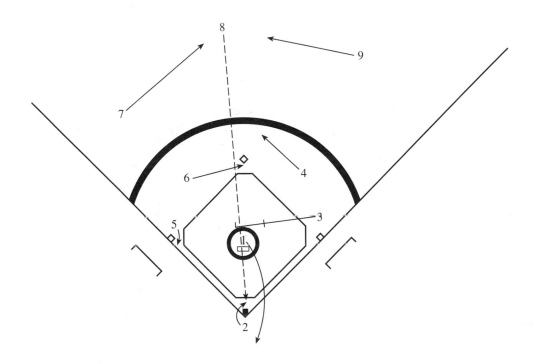

Situation #11

Single to Center Field with Runners on First and Second Bases or Bases Loaded

Player:

1. Take position halfway between home plate and third; back up base where the play develops. Must observe action and throw.

2. Protect home plate.

3. React to become cutoff man to home plate.

4. Cover second base.

5. Cover third base.

6. Observe action and become a possible cutoff man with the throw to third base.

7. Back up center fielder

8. Make a hard throw through either cutoff man. React to what you see and hear from teammates.

9. Move in to infield.

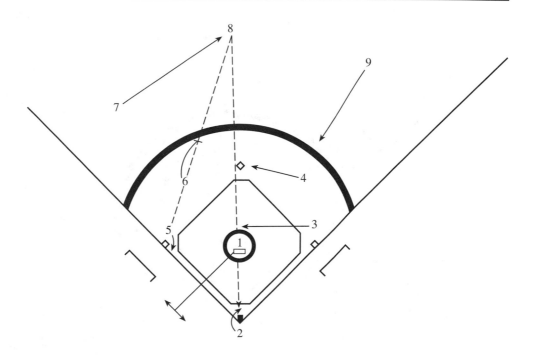

Situation #12

Fly Ball to Right or Center Field with Runners on First and Third Bases, or Bases Loaded

Player:

1. Move to back up home plate.

2. Remain at home to protect it.

3. Become the cutoff man in either case.

4. Move to cover first base.

5. Protect third base.

6. Cover second base.

7. Move into infield.

8. **and 9.** Move toward fly ball or, if fielding ball, make strong throw through the cutoff man to plate. Direction of throw depends on distance of fly ball, score, and so on.

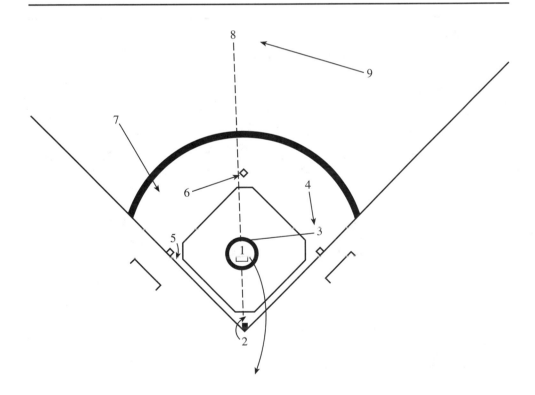

Situation #13

Single to Right Field with Bases Empty

Player:

1. Go to a position halfway between mound and second base.

2. Remain at home.

3. Observe that the runner tags first base while making the turn; stay to cover first base.

4. Covers second base; take throw from right fielder.

5. Remain to protect third-base area.

6. Back up right fielder's throw to second base.

7. Move in toward third base.

8. Back up right fielder.

9. Make low, strong throw to second base.

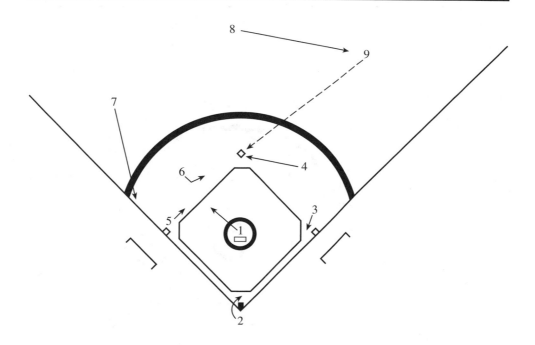

Situation #14

Single to Right Field with Runner on First Base or Runners on First and Third Bases

Player:

1. Move to back up third base; line up with throw.

2. Remain to protect home plate.

3. Remain to cover first base and observe runner tagging base.

4. Remain to cover second base and observe runner tagging base.

5. Cover third base.

6. Be the cutoff man between right fielder and third base.

7. Move in toward third base.

8. Back up right fielder.

9. Make strong, low throw through cutoff man to third base.

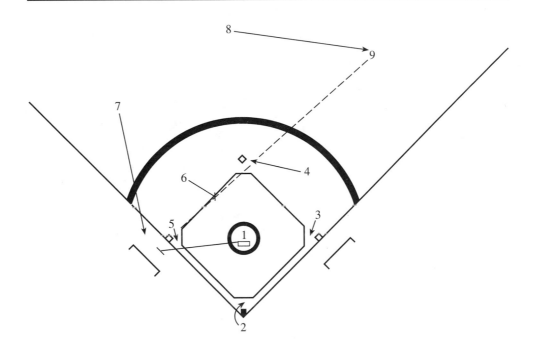

Situation #15

Single to Right Field with Runner on Second Base or Runners on Second and Third Bases

Player:

1. Move to back up home plate.

2. Protect home plate.

3. Be the cutoff man between right field and home plate; take position about 45 feet from home plate.

4. Move to cover first base.

5. Protect third base; possible cut; play at third base.

6. Protect second base; possible cut; play at second base.

7. Move in toward third base.

8. Back up right fielder.

9. Make strong throw through cutoff man to plate.

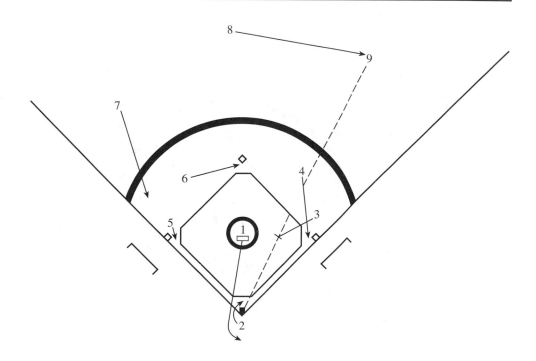

Situation #16

Single to Right Field with Runners on First and Second Bases or Bases Loaded*

Player:

1. Assume position halfway between third and home; react to play.

2. Protect home plate.

3. Be cutoff man if throw is made to plate.

4. Cover second base.

5. Cover third base.

6. Be cutoff man for throw to third base.

7. Move in to assist; back up third base.

8. Back up right fielder.

*9. Can do one of many things. All depend on score and number of outs. Some basics to observe: Never allow tying or winning run as a result of going to third with less than two outs. Give up the runs to keep tying run at second. Don't make a foolish throw.

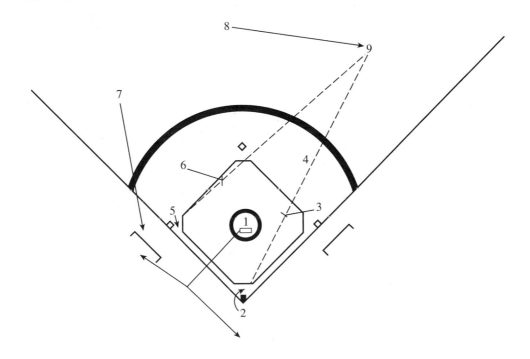

Situation #17

Double, Possible Triple, to Right Center Field with No One on Base, Man on Second or Third Base, or Men on Second and Third Bases

Player:

1. Back up third; get deep.

2. Protect home plate.

3. Trail the runner (original batter) to second base; cover bag for possible play at that base.

4. Go out to center field, line up between third base and fielder of ball. You are the relay man.

5. Cover third base.

6. Be the trail abut 30 feet behind the second baseman; line up with third base.

7. Move in toward third base.

8. Get to ball and make strong throw to relay man.

9. Back up center fielder.

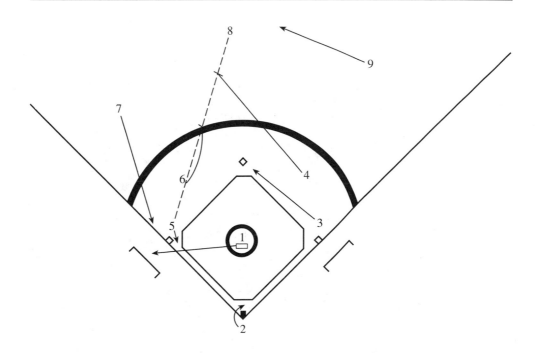

Situation #18

Double, Possible Triple, to Right Center Field with Men on First and Second Bases or Bases Loaded

Player:

1. Go halfway between third and home; see where the throw is coming and then back up the proper base.

2. Cover home plate.

3. Trail runner and move to middle of diamond for cutoff.

4. Be the cutoff man.

5. Cover third base.

6. Trail the relay man.

7. Move into area behind third base.

8. and 9. Go after the ball and make strong throw to relay man, who in turn throws to third or home.

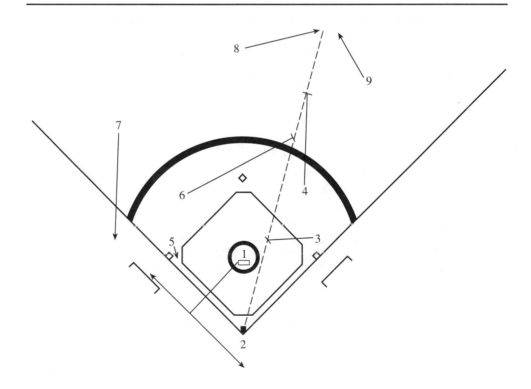

Situation #19

Double, Possible Triple, Down Right Field Line with No One on Bases

Player:

1. Back up third base.

2. Protect home plate.

3. Trail runner to second base; possible tag play.

4. Be the first relay man (double relay)

5. Cover third base.

6. Be the trailer relay man (double relay)

7. Move into area behind third base.

8. Back up right fielder.

9. Make strong throw to first relay man.

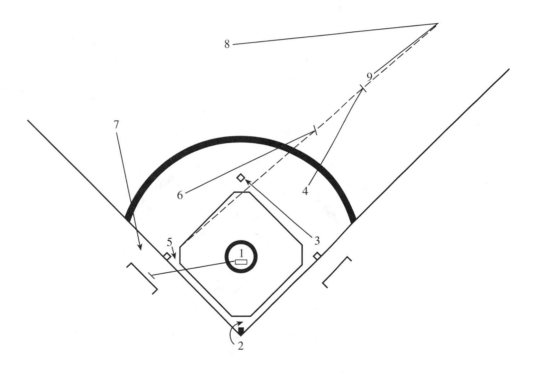

Situation #20

Triple, Possible Home Run Down Right-Field Line with Man on First Base

Player:

1. Go halfway between home and third; see where throw is going; react to play.

2. Cover home plate.

3. Trail second baseman by 30 feet.

4. Be relay man; go into right field; line up between right fielder and home. Distance out is determined by where right fielder fields ball.

5. Cover third base.

6. Be cutoff man.

7. Move in toward third base.

8. Back up right fielder.

9. Make strong throw to relay man.

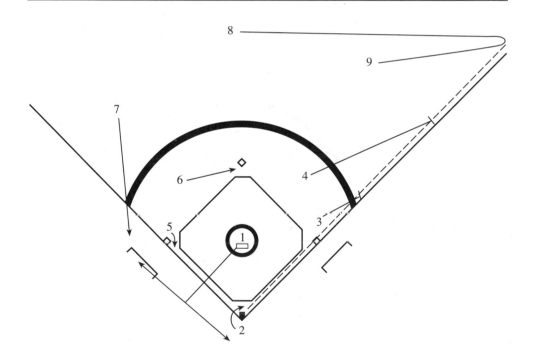

DEFENSIVE ASSIGNMENTS ON BUNT SITUATIONS
Defense Situation #1

Runner on First Base

Player:

1. Break toward home plate after delivering the ball.

2. Field all bunts possible; call the play; cover third base when third baseman fields the bunt close to home plate.

3. Cover the area between first base and the pitcher's mound.

4. Cover first base; cheat by shortening position.

5. Cover the area between third and the pitcher's mound.

6. Cover second base.

7. Move in toward second-base area.

8. Back up second base.

9. Back up first base.

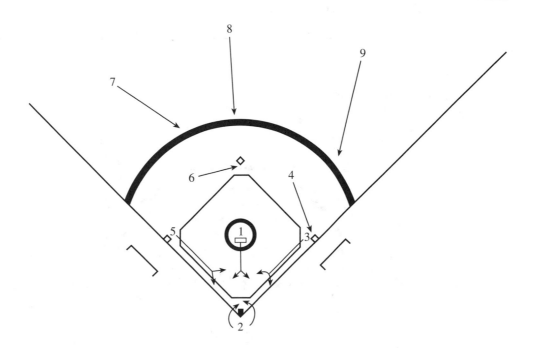

DEFENSIVE ASSIGNMENTS ON BUNT SITUATIONS

Defense Situation #2

Runners on First and Second Bases

Player:

1. Break toward the third-base line upon delivering the ball.

2. Field bunts in front of home plate; *call the play*.

3. Be responsible for all balls in the area between first base and in a direct line from the mound to home plate.

4. Cover first base.

5. Take a position on the edge of the grass. Call the pitcher off when the third baseman is going to field the bunt.

6. Hold runner close to the base before the pitch; cover second base.

7. Back up third base.

8. Back up second base.

9. Back up first base. First objective is to retire the runner at third base, but one runner *must* be retired.

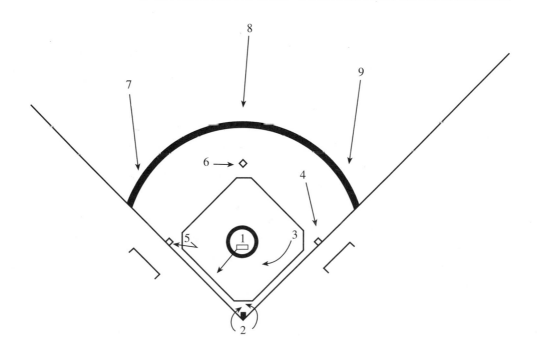

DEFENSIVE ASSIGNMENTS ON BUNT SITUATIONS
Defense Situation #3
Runners on First and Second Bases

Player:

1. Break toward the plate.

2. Field bunts in front of plate or *call the play.*

3. Charge toward the plate.

4. Cover first base.

5. Charge toward the plate.

6. Bluff runner back to second; then race to cover third.

7. Back up third base.

8. Back up second base.

9. Back up first base.

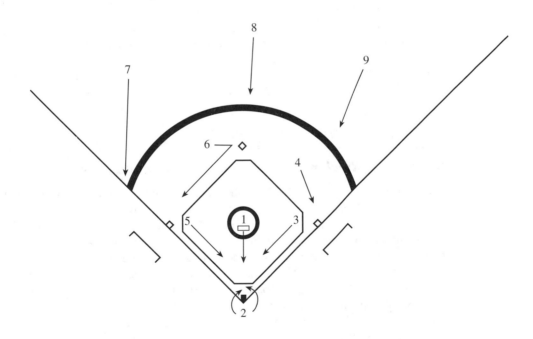

THE PRINCIPLES OF THE RUNDOWN PLAY

Every team must have a planned defense for a rundown situation. Players must understand the following principles before game situations are presented.

- Keep the number of throws to a minimum. Try to make only one throw.
- Run the base runner back to the base from which he came.
- Chase the runner as hard as you can, but be under control and ready for any move the runner attempts to make to avoid a tag.
- Chase the runner on either the inside or the outside of the imaginary baseline. Do not throw over the runner.
- Keep the ball high and in the throwing hand. Do not fake with the arm. A strong dart-type throw should be made when the receiving defensive player calls for the ball.
- The receiving defensive player should shorten the distance between himself and the runner by moving toward the runner and away from the base behind him.
- The receiving defensive player gives a command to the chaser when he wants the ball to be thrown to him (*Now, Me, Ball,* and so on). The coach selects the verbal command the team will use.
- The release command is given as the runner gets closer to the receiving player (approximately 15 feet). The receiving player steps up toward the runner to receive the ball and makes the tag.
- Defensive players must learn to stay under control and force the base runner to commit himself.

THE ROTATING RUNDOWN METHOD

Situation 1: Rundown between First and Second Bases

When a runner is caught off first base, the pitcher immediately breaks toward first base and positions himself behind the base. The shortstop runs to cover second base, and the second baseman runs toward first base to get behind the runner. The first baseman runs the runner about halfway to second base and throws the ball to the shortstop. After he throws the ball, he continues toward second base by rotating to the right side of the runner.

The shortstop receives the throw and runs toward first base as hard as he can. As the runner is approaching the second baseman, the shortstop throws the ball to the second baseman. Because the runner is running at full speed, it is impossible for him to stop and start back in the opposite direction before being tagged out. The second baseman receives the throw and tags the runner. If the tag is not made, the shortstop continues toward first base to be in position if the rundown continues. As the rundown develops, the center fielder moves into a backup position behind second base. The pitcher should not get involved in the play unless he has to. He backs up other players or bases in case of any bad throws.

Situation 2: Rundown between Second and Third Bases

As soon as the runner is caught off second base, the pitcher breaks toward third base and positions himself behind the base. The second baseman or shortstop, depending on who has the ball, chases the base runner approximately halfway to third base and throws the ball to the third baseman. After he throws the ball, he continues on to third base by rotating to the right side.

The third baseman now runs the base runner toward second base as hard as he can. As the runner approaches the fielder covering second base, the third baseman makes the throw when the fielder calls for the ball. The fielder receives the throw, steps up, and makes the tag. The third baseman continues toward second base after he throws by keeping to the right side of the runner in case the rundown continues. As the play develops, the center fielder positions himself so that he can back up any errant throws.

Situation 3: Rundown between Third Base and Home Plate

As soon as the runner is caught off third base, the pitcher breaks toward home plate unless the ball is hit directly back to him; then he runs toward the runner. The shortstop goes behind third base, and the first baseman comes toward home plate. The third baseman runs the base runner about halfway to home plate and then gives the ball to the catcher. The catcher then runs the base runner back toward third base and gives the ball to the shortstop, who is moving up to make the tag. Again the rotation system is followed: players always rotate to the base to which they throw.

If the rundown starts with the pitcher having the ball and if the runner is well off base, the pitcher runs straight at the runner and forces him to commit himself. The pitcher should give the ball up immediately and let the infielders continue the rundown.

THE ONE-THROW RUNDOWN METHOD

The simple philosophy for a rundown play is to complete it with one throw. With only one throw, there is less chance of error, less chance that other base runners will advance, and less chance that fielders will run into base runners and have interference called.

In the rundown, the infielder who has the ball immediately runs at full speed toward the runner, trying to get the runner moving at full speed toward the next base or tagger. The infielder holds the ball above shoulder level in the throwing position, which allows the tagger to see the ball at all times. The infielder runs outside the left shoulder of the runner if he is a left-handed thrower and outside the right shoulder if he is a right-handed thrower. This prevents the ball from being thrown over the runner's head, thus blocking the view of the ball by the runner.

The tagger receiving the ball closes the distance between the runner and the other infielder by moving toward the runner. When the tagger sees that the runner is coming at him at full speed, he calls out and takes a step up to receive the ball. When the infielder with the ball hears the call, he uses a dart-type throw and gives the ball to the tagger, who receives the ball and makes the tag.

The tagger must be careful not to let the runner get too close to him before calling for the ball. If this were to happen, the runner could pass him or force him to catch the ball and try to tag the runner in the same motion. The tagger must also make sure that he does not call for the ball too soon and give the runner a chance to stop and reverse direction. The right timing is very important in a rundown play. It takes a lot of practice to make it work.

Remember: when a player is caught in a rundown, the defensive team must record an out. Don't let him get away.

DEFENSING THE FIRST-AND-THIRD DOUBLE STEAL

A well-organized team should coordinate the various play options and individual skills used to defense the first-and-third double steal. Let's look at the major situations where this double steal can be applied.

Situation 1: Defensing the Straight Steal

The runner on first base breaks toward second base as the pitcher delivers the ball to home plate. The runner either goes all the way and slides into second base or goes three-quarters of the way, stops, and looks to get in a rundown situation. The runner on third base can either break for home when he sees that the ball will go by the pitcher to second base or wait for the runner to get into the rundown and try to score while that play is being made.

To defense this, the catcher quickly looks at the runner on third base before releasing the ball to second base. If the runner is too far off the base, he can throw the ball to third base. If he throws the ball to second base, the infielder covering the base should be one step in front of the base, ready either to tag the incoming runner or to cut the ball and throw it to home plate.

If a rundown situation occurs, the infielder who takes the throw either walks or uses a controlled run at the runner coming from first base. This allows him to watch both the runner at third base and the runner on whom he is closing in. The first baseman is closing the distance between himself and the runner so a quick tag can be made.

The following options should be practiced in defensing the straight double steal.

1. The catcher throws right back to the pitcher, hoping to catch the runner breaking on the catcher's throwing movement.
2. The shortstop or second baseman moves into a cutoff position between the pitcher's mound and second base. The player covering second base watches the runner at third base. If he breaks for home, he yells, "Cut," and the ball is cut and thrown to home plate to record the out. If the runner does not break, the player at second base lets the ball come through and tags the runner coming into second base.
3. The catcher throws the ball to the shortstop, who is coming straight toward home plate from his position, so that he will receive the ball at the edge of the infield grass halfway between second and third bases.
4. The catcher throws the ball directly to third base.

Situation 2: Defensing the Early Break

The runner on first base breaks toward second base during the pitcher's delivery. To defense this situation, the pitcher steps back off the rubber. He looks at the runner on third base, freezes him, then gives the ball up to the second baseman, who has now positioned himself in front of second base. From here the second baseman can throw the ball home if the runner from third breaks, or he can start the rundown of the runner between first and second bases.

Situation 3: Defensing the Delayed Steal

The runner on first base breaks toward second base just as the ball is entering the hitting zone. At this point, all eyes are on the hitter. The runner is hoping to catch the defense sleeping—hoping that they will not see him make the break to second base. The runner on first base can also break just as the catcher is about to return the ball to the pitcher. The runner is keying on a catcher who drops to his knees and throws from that position. To throw to second base, the catcher must double pump, get off his knees, and throw. This play is also aimed at the shortstop and second baseman who drop their heads after the pitch or who turn to the outfield and give them the number of outs.

To defense any of these situations, all infielders must recognize the possibility of a delayed steal any time there is a first-and-third situation. As soon as the ball passes the hitter, one of the middle infielders goes immediately to second base and positions himself two steps in front of the base, facing home plate. If the runner breaks from first base, the catcher has a stationary target. The catcher must work on his mechanics and not get into the habit of going to his knees unless it is to block a ball in the dirt.

Situation 4: Defensing Runners Tagging Up on Foul Pop-Ups behind First and Third Bases

The runner at first base tags up on a foul pop-up behind first or third base. The third baseman and shortstop or the second baseman and first baseman go for the ball in their respective areas. If the ball is caught, the runner on first base tags up and heads for second base. The runner on third base tags up, shuffles off the base, and waits to see where the ball is thrown. If the ball is thrown to second base, the runner on third base tries to score.

To defense this situation, a cutoff man must shorten the throws. If the ball is hit down the first-base line, the shortstop positions himself between first and second bases. The infielder catching the ball immediately throws the ball to the shortstop. If the runner from third base tries to score, the shortstop cuts the ball and throws it home. If the runner at third base doesn't break, the shortstop tries to tag the runner coming from first base to second base.

If the ball is hit down the third-base line, the pitcher runs halfway between third base and home plate, about 5 feet in foul territory. The infielder who catches the ball immediately throws it to the pitcher, who checks the runner on third base and throws to second base in an attempt to record the out there.

Remember: the main objective in defensing this type of play is not to let the run score.

Situation 5: Defensing Runners Tagging Up on Foul Pop-Ups to the Catcher behind Home Plate

A foul pop-up is hit toward the backstop behind the catcher. The runner on first base tags up when the catcher catches the ball. The runner on third base tags up and comes off the base slowly toward home plate. He waits to see whether the catcher throws to second base. In this situation, the pitcher covers home plate when the catcher chases the foul ball. If the catcher throws to second base from the backstop without a cutoff man in position, the runner from third base might walk home.

To defense this situation, the shortstop goes to a cutoff position in front of the pitcher's mound. The catcher immediately throws the ball to the shortstop, who checks the runner at third base or throws to second base in an attempt to record the out there.

Situation 6: Defensing the Intentional Pickoff at First Base

The runner at first base takes a larger than usual lead, enticing the pitcher to throw. On the pitcher's first move, the runner breaks for second base. When the first baseman throws to second base, the runner on third base breaks for home plate.

To defense this situation, a right-handed pitcher lifts his lead leg and steps toward third base. This freezes the runner or picks him off if he is too far off the base. If the runner on third base does not break, the pitcher turns and throws to either first or second base to make a play. A left-handed pitcher quickly steps back off the rubber and makes a quick snap throw to first base.

Team Defensive Drills

DRILL 10.1.   Offensive/Defensive First-and-Third Variations

Purpose: To work on the execution of first-and-third situations, both offensively and defensively.

Area Required: Infield area.

Equipment Needed: Helmets for runners, bases, and baseballs.

Procedure: Runners are at first and third bases (they will continually rotate). All infielders are at their positions, and a pitcher is on the mound. The pitcher delivers the pitch to home plate, and the runners execute a variety of first-and-third double steals. The defense communicates according to individual reads and coverages. The coach can give signs to the runners while the infielders turn their backs to the coach so they do not know what play will be run. This is a good way to review signs with the players. There is no sliding, and rundowns can be included in the drill. Pitchers, infielders, and runners rotate so that everyone gets a chance to practice.

This drill can also be used to work on defensing the foul pop-ups behind first and third and the foul pop-up behind home plate.

DRILL 10.2.   Defensive Responsibility

Purpose: To review defensive responsibilities with all players at one time.

Area Required: Baseball field, or drill can be adjusted to a smaller area.

Equipment Needed: None.

Procedure: All players take the field at their respective positions. The coach shouts out a situation (for example, base hit to left field with a runner on first base), or a play (for example, timing pickoff at second base). All players react to each situation or play. Because no baseball is used, the players are concerned only with their positioning during the play. This drill can help review every key defensive situation and all plays in a short time.

11

THE COACH AND TEAM MANAGEMENT

DEVELOPING TEAM CHARACTER

A team develops its character and style of play from the leadership provided by the coach. Players are aggressive, confident, fundamentally sound, and not intimidated because they have assumed the personality of their coach, who exemplifies these strengths. When spectators, opposing coaches, and players talk about good teams, their statements are always about how good teams conduct themselves and how they perform under pressure.

The personality of a team starts with the man in charge. He is the one who sets the tone through his example, his behavior, his knowledge of the game and how it is played, his understanding of the rules, his give-and-take with his players, and perhaps most important, his honesty with everyone. The good teams are there for the playoffs every year. A team that shows up once in a while, because of an outstanding player or two, lacks the foundation and consistency that good programs have year in and year out. The coach brings together individuals who are seeking the sound teaching and coaching that will make them good individual players and a good team. A consistent program has the strong foundation and leadership that bring together individuals who want to succeed. A winning tradition starts with a strong leader who, in turn, selects individuals who will strive for the goals that are set.

Let's look at one of the most difficult tasks of a coach: the selection and evaluation of individuals for team membership. A coach's philosophy and character come into play in this selection process, and the coach shows his coaching qualities and style in the process. What is he looking for? The best player? The best athlete? Individuals who will fit his system best? These are just some of the qualities that a coach takes into consideration when selecting a team. Remember, we all must determine which qualifications are best suited to our situation and try to be successful in using them. A coach learns from his decisions and makes adjustments if needed.

Following are the characteristics of most successful coaches.

1. A knowledge of the game, its strategies, and the rules that govern the sport.
2. The ability to teach the fundamentals of the game. A coach must be a good teacher.

3. The ability to motivate and stimulate players to perform to their potential.
4. The ability to understand and coach young men in today's environment. There can be only one person in charge, and it must be the coach. A good coach must listen to and understand what others have to say; but the final decisions are his, and he takes full responsibility for them.
5. The courage to carry out his convictions and to guide his players to be good athletes as well as fine young men.
6. The ability to set rules that apply to all and that can enforced for the good of the team.

Never make a rule that you cannot keep.

The areas of concern in the team selection and evaluation process are many. Sometimes candidates have selected a position that they really can't play. Don't be overly concerned about their choice of position, but look for individuals with good skills. Following are some desirable characteristics of candidates.

1. Good physical skills such as coordination, good hands, soft hands, rhythm, and good eye-hand coordination.
2. Good throwing ability, with strength and accuracy. How often do you see a knowledgeable coach turn an individual with a strong arm into a good pitcher or an outstanding outfielder?
3. Good running speed—an asset both offensively and defensively.
4. Good batting skills such as: quiet hands, still head and eyes, short stride or at least a stride toward the pitcher, level swing, strength.
5. Mental and physical awareness. How does he handle a difficult and stressful situation? Can he mature as a player? Sometimes an individual cannot mature as a player, even with practice.
6. Likelihood of being a team player. Can he fit in? Does he want to fit in?
7. Willingness to work on improving the skills that he has. Does he have the right attitude for success in baseball? It is not an easy game to play. It requires the ability to control one's actions in the face of either success or failure.

When you have decided on your selection process and have selected your team, you must begin to put it all together. Start with strength down the middle—that is, good pitching, good catching, a strong shortstop/second base combination, and a good center fielder. It is not difficult to find the bodies, but you must now teach and coach these young men so that they are well schooled in the fundamentals of the game.

Don't expect your players to perform as champions if you have not taught them how to react to various situations that are basic to the game of baseball. Don't expect them to do something that they are not capable of doing. You are in control when it comes to teaching and coaching them. Everyone is different, and as a coach, you must know how much each player can absorb and how much each can do. Some players learn faster than others; you must know who they are and coach them accordingly.

Be a good listener. Nothing turns off a player faster than cutting him off before he has completed a question. Be aware of when you are using the time to coach and make adjustments and/or corrections. The proper time is when both player and coach are open to both criticisms and cures.

Remember that no one has a lock on success in baseball. If anything, baseball makes everyone human. We must all learn to be patient with both success and failure in this game.

TEAM PREPARATION

The following list was published in the February 1966 issue of *Athletic Journal*. It was written by Donald C. Bennicke, the baseball coach at Granville High School in Milwaukee, Wisconsin. You can add to or substract from the groupings listed as you see fit. The important point is that you have before you information that can help you sort out the skills that must be developed by both coaches and players, both before and after the season.

Group 1 Equipment. Taking care of equipment, team rules, daily diet and meals.

Group 2 Conditioning and training. Pregame warm-up, proper dress, signal or sign system.

Group 3 Various throws. Fielding grounders, catching pop-up flies, playing the sun field.

Group 4 Baserunning philosophy. Sliding and tagging up, baseline coaches.

Group 5 Science of batting. Selecting a bat, gripping the bat, stance, proper bunting position, swing.

Group 6 Playing first base. Playing second base, playing third base, playing short-stop.

Group 7 Playing the outfield. Science of the outfield, playing the catching position, art of pitching.

Group 8 Covering bases. Tagging runners, lining up throws, backing up plays.

Group 9 Sacrifice bunt. Bunting for base hit, running to first base, squeeze play.

Group 10 Basic windup and delivery. Pitcher's warm-up, basic pitches, set pitching stance.

Group 11 Leading off first base. Stealing second base, leading off second base, stealing third base.

Group 12 Leading off third base. Stealing home, basic offensive strategy, batting order.

Group 13 Swinging the bat. Batting stride, hitting to opposite field, emotional factors in batting.

Group 14 Special pitches. Pitcher as fielder, developing pitching control, battery signals.

Group 15 Footwork of first baseman. Throwing by catcher, types of defensive situations, defensive drills.

Group 16 Rundown play. Making double play, holding runners on base, pickoff plays at second base.

Coach Bennicke also stated the following:

Groups 1 and 2 are concerned with getting ready to play the game.

Groups 3, 4, and 5 cover basics in fielding, throwing, hitting, and running.

Groups 6 and 7 have to do with playing individual positions.

Groups 8, 9, 11, and 12 deal with the fine points that tighten up the basic offense and defense.

Groups 10 and 14 work with the pitching staff.

Group 13 follows Group 5 to emphasize some points of batting.

Groups 15 and 16 also follow up the basics in each area.

Now we have the menu. We can add to it as it suits us, and we can subtract from it as well. Let's look at a way to add to a group.

Group 2: Conditioning and training. The philosophy of a pitcher's conditioning program can be part of this group. What do you want the pitchers to understand about conditioning? What are the purposes of the long toss and the short toss, and when do you want the pitchers to perform them? The same can be asked about weight training and endurance work.

Group 13: Swinging the bat. The philosophy of hitting, from bat selection to follow-through, can be incorporated into this group. For example, head should be quiet and still and follow the ball into the catcher's glove when player is not swinging. Coaching cues can be introduced. For example, *on the swing, the chin goes from shoulder to shoulder,* or *look at the pitcher's point of release to see the ball more quickly and longer.*

As a coach plans his indoor workouts, he now has information to draw from in organizing his team practices. Each skill to be taught should be broken down systematically so that the coach can emphasize the points that he wishes his players to learn. Remember: this philosophy includes all aspects of getting a team to perform at its best and covers all possible learning of skills with the facilities available. A practice session should be a quality experience for everyone. Practice time can be difficult, depending on the time of year and location, but when it is spent constructively, everyone gains.

INDOOR PRACTICE ORGANIZATION

When a coach prepares a team for indoor practice, his philosophy is followed throughout the planning. As stated previously, this is where a team starts to develop character. The following factors should be considered.

1. What priorities must be met during the indoor workouts?
   a. Team goals have to be established.
   b. Individual goals must be met by the coach and the player.
2. How can the available facilities be used to the fullest?
   a. Time availability.
   b. Space availability.

Indoor Drills

DRILL 11.1.   Indoor Circus Drill

Purpose: To repeat drills that deal with game situations, to keep everyone involved, and to practice correctly.

Area Required: Indoor gymnasium.

Equipment Needed: Two protective screens, baseballs, catchers' equipment, fungos.

Procedure: **A.** All drills start with a pitch.
  B. Work catchers in full gear.
  C. A screen is needed for some drills.
  D. Two fungo hitters are needed.

There are 7 parts to this drill.

1. Covering first base (3-1).
   Pitchers: Throw home, then cover first base.
   Catchers: Receive pitch and throw to second base, with shortstop and second baseman covering.
   Third baseman: Catch ground ball and throw back to fungo hitter on right side. (See Figure 11.1.)
2. Double Play (3-6-1) with runners on first and second bases.
   Pitchers: Throw home from stretch, cover first base.

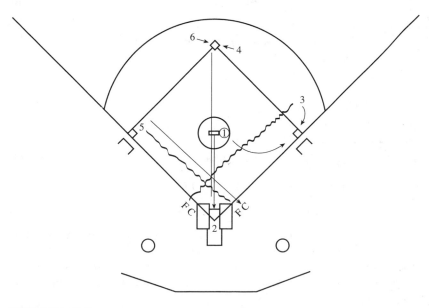

FIGURE 11.1

Catchers: Throw to third base.

Fungo ball to first base.

Shortstop: Receive ball from first baseman and return throw to pitcher covering first base.

3. Double play (1-6-3, 1-4-3, 5-2-3) (screen needed).

Pitchers: Field ball back from fungo on left side and throw to second base. Middle infielders give signals as to who is covering second base. Fungo ball to third base from right side; third baseman throws home.

Catchers: Take throw from third base and throw to first base.

Middle infielders: Take throws from pitcher at second base.

4. Double play (1-2-3, 5-4-3).

Pitchers: Take fungo ball and throw home (left-side fungo).

Catchers: Take ball from pitcher; throw to first base (screen needed).

Third basemen: Take fungo ball and go to second, then to first base (right-side fungo).

Middle infielders: Take throws at second base.

5. Double play (4-6-3, 6-4-3).

Pitchers: Field bunt rolled to left side by coach and throw to third base.

Catchers: Pickoffs at first base with a ball thrown by pitcher (screen needed).

Fungo ball to second base from right, work on 4-6-3 double play.

Can reverse the drill with 6-4-3 double play. Pitchers go to first base with bunt.

Middle infielders: Work at second base.

6. Bunt defense, man on first base, regular defense.

Ball rolled by coach on left side.

All infielders: React to a regular defense on bunt 5-1-3 charge, shortstop covers second base, second baseman covers first.

Runners: Work on bunt leads, react to ball.

7. Bunt Defense, man on first and second bases, regular defense.

Ball rolled by coach on left side.

Pitchers: Make play at third or first base.

Third basemen: Learn when to charge and make play at first.

Can work special bunt defense off 7 and 6.

DRILL 11.2.   High Hop/Short Hop

Purpose: To work on infielder's approach to high/short hop ground balls.

Area Required: Confined space of gymnasium or field.

Equipment Needed: Rubber covered balls or tennis balls.

Procedure: Player is 10–15 yards from coach. Coach throws ball to ground to cause a high bounce or hop. The fielder judges the hop and *must* catch the ball on the short hop. This skill should be mastered by all infielders because it is a common occurrence in ball games. Footwork, approach, and other infield techniques are practiced simultaneously.

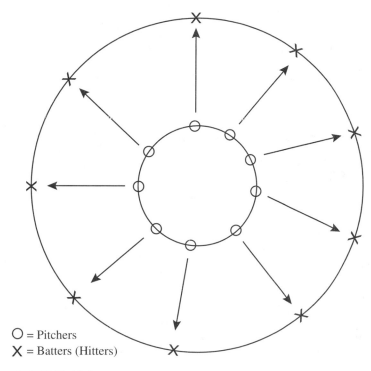

O = Pitchers
X = Batters (Hitters)

FIGURE 11.2

DRILL 11.3. Batting Practice Wheel

Purpose: To work on simultaneous mass indoor or outdoor hitting.

Area Required: Varies, depending on age of hitters.

Equipment Needed: Bats and Wiffle balls.

Procedure: Put Wiffle balls in center of wheel with pitchers (O); they throw to hitters (X). A number of throws is established. The group picks up the balls at the end of the throws, and players switch roles. (See Figure 11.2.)

HOW TO GET THE MOST OUT OF DAILY WORKOUTS

It is essential that a team come to the field prepared every day—not only the players, but the coach as well. The daily practice schedule should be posted every day before practice begins. Let's look at some tips for organizing a constructive practice.

1. As stated earlier, the daily practice schedule should be posted.
2. Every team member should be involved in using essential skills during a game situation.

3. A check-off list of skills and drills that must be covered should be a guide for the coaching staff. This check-off list should contain both individual and team skills.
4. Location, time of year, and team makeup will prioritize practice.
5. Practices must be kept moving. Practice the way you want your team to play.
6. Instruction in the proper procedure should precede drills that require special technique.

Typical Plan for a Daily Practice Session

1:00 P.M. All team members are on field for practice.

1:00–1:20 P.M. Stretching exercises are conducted in the outfield by team members.

1:20–1:25 P.M. All team members take two laps around the field.

1:25–1:35 P.M. Players catch, using proper technique in their throwing and catching. Outfielders practice the throws that they will use in a game. Throws should be over the top, and the grip on the ball should be across the seams. Pitchers practice balance in their delivery by pausing in their pivot before throwing to one another. Catchers and infielders practice getting the ball away quickly by using quick, snappy throws and proper footwork.

1:35–1:50 P.M. Individual position practice. Players have a checklist for their position. This time allows the coach to work on individual techniques with the players. The pitchers can be used in these drills as fungo hitters or feeders.

1:50–2:05 P.M. Pitchers work on mound drills. Infielders and catchers are also included in these drills. Outfielders begin playing pepper and performing various tee work to develop hand-eye coordination and agility. This is also a good time to use various soft-toss drills.

2:05–2:20 P.M. A particular team defense can be practiced now (first and third straight steal, both offense and defense).

2:20–2:30 P.M. Team relay and cutoff practice.

2:30–to end. Batting practice. Batting can be set up in many different ways: position hitting or group hitting based on time or swings or number of contacts are just a few. Pitchers who are not throwing should be hitting fungos to the infielders. Infielders should be in their positions when not hitting, playing the ball off the bat at all times. At the very end of practice, a good conditioning drill can be used, in which players run around the bases to build up their endurance and practice the correct baserunning procedures.

Drills That Can Be Used in Practice

DRILL 11.4.   Thirty-Minute Team Drill

Purpose: To reinforce prior teaching and coaching (twice a week).

Area Required: Full field.

Equipment Needed: Individual and team equipment.

Procedure:

2 minutes—Infielders and catchers field slow rollers.
2 minutes—Infielders and catchers have a play at the plate.

2 minutes—Catchers have pickoffs at first base.

Middle infielders have communication on ball up the middle.

Third basemen have fly ball over head/tag plays (decoy).

3 minutes—Pitcher cover first base.

Catchers have pickoff at third base.

Middle infielders do quick-hands drill in a circle.

3 minutes—Pitchers cover first base with throws from second baseman and first baseman.

Shortstop and third basemen have ground balls in the hole.

Catchers catch for coaches.

3 minutes—Pitchers, first basemen, and middle infielders have 3-6-1 play.

Catchers and third basemen, have pop-up communication (balls are thrown by coach).

2 minutes—Pitchers, middle infielders, and first basemen have comebackers (1-6-3, 1-4-3).

Catchers and third basemen continue pop-ups.

1 minute —Pitchers have no-step throw to first base.

Middle infielders have forehand and backhand.

Third basemen have forehand and backhand.

Catchers have dry block.

3 minutes—Pitchers, infielders, and catchers have bunts with runners on first and second bases (extra outfielders and pitchers run bases).

3 minutes—Pitchers and middle infielders have pickoffs at second base.

Third basemen work on short hops by throwing 50 feet away from bag.

First basemen work on short hops by throwing about 50 feet away from the bag (relay to third).

Catchers are framing pitches.

3 minutes—Pitchers have pickoffs to first base.

Catchers have blocking balls.

Infielders have tag plays.

3 minutes—Infielders and outfielders have communication.

DRILL 11.5. Total Offensive Drill

Purpose: To have all bases covered during live batting practice. This keeps players from waiting to hit. The more a player focuses and is involved, the better he becomes.

Area Required: Baseball field.

Equipment Needed: All equipment needed for regular practice session.

Procedure: Load the bases. All base runners react to hit ball. The runner on second base plays the hit as if there were no runner on third base. The runner on third base reacts to the ball off the bat (fly ball, line drive, or ground ball). The pitcher does not acknowledge the runner at third base, only those at first and second bases. The same drill can be used starting at first base. The pitcher acknowledges the runner at first base only. The third-base coach is involved. This gets the players used to him, and he learns the strong and weak points of the base runners.

DRILL 11.6.   Pride Drill

Purpose: To create excitement and pride in a do-or-die situation.

Area Required: Baseball field.

Equipment Needed: All equipment needed for regular practice session.

Procedure: This is an outdoor drill, done periodically at the end of practice. The situation: last of the ninth inning, winning run on second base, right-handed batter at the plate. The coach soft tosses to the batter. The right-handed batter must pull the ball to the left side of the infield. If the shortstop or third baseman fields the ball, he throws the batter out at first base. The players try to keep the ball in the infield. If the ball goes through the infield, the center fielder or left fielder must throw the runner out at the plate.

The same situation is set up for a left-handed hitter. The left-handed hitter must pull the ball to the right side of the field. If the second baseman or first baseman fields the ball, he throws the batter out at first base. If the ball goes through the infield, the center fielder or right fielder must throw the runner out at the plate.

DRILL 11.7.   Outfield Backup Drill

Purpose: To work on team defense.

Area Required: Baseball field.

Equipment Needed: All equipment needed for regular practice sessions.

Procedure: Put a whole defensive team on field, outfielders in right and left fields. Pitchers rotate in after a specified number of pitches. All other players can act as base runners at home plate. The coach then hits a fungo ball in one of three ways: (1) a ground ball to the third baseman, (2) a slow roller to the third baseman, or (3) a bunt with the catcher or pitcher fielding the ball. When the ball is fielded by the third baseman and thrown across to the first baseman, the latter allows the ball to get by. The right fielder, second baseman, and catcher must communicate and call the ball to keep the base runner from going to third base. The left fielder backs up third base, anticipating the throw. Outfielders switch positions every 15 minutes.

DRILL 11.8.   Situation Batting Practice

Purpose: To provide maximum hitting practice under semi-live conditions. All areas of the offensive game are practiced. Also, a majority of defensive situations are practiced under semi-live conditions, with players in primary and secondary positions.

Area Required: Full field.

Equipment Needed: All equipment needed for regular practice sessions.

Procedure: 1. Divide sixteen position players into four groups.
2. The hitting group supplies base runners if needed.
3. Hitters get three or six outs, whichever is appropriate.
4. Points are scored on successes or runs.

5. Defense plays line. If a coach is used as pitcher, the pitchers stand behind the screen and back up the appropriate bases.
6. Various offensive situations are covered as listed below.

Example: Numbers next to names represent defensive positions.

Group 1			*Group 2*			*Group 3*			*Group 4*		
Matthew	8,	9	Kevin	7,	9	Dan	6,	4	Michael	6,	5
Phil	4,	6	Don	3,	7	Fred	2,	5	Joe	2	
John	9,	8	Bob	2,	3	Andy	3,	7	Jim	6,	4
Howie	7,	3	Willie	5,	6	Stu	8,	9	Scott	9,	8

Group 1: Hitting: Specific situations are dictated by signs from the third-base coach (for example, steal).
Group 2: Primary position.
Group 3: Secondary position.
Group 4: Hitting drills (Tunnel): Rotate from hitting to primary position, to secondary position, to hitting drill area.

Hitting Situations Covered

1. Runner on first (3 outs)
   Hit and run
   Sacrifice bunt
   Straight steal
2. Runner on second (3 outs)
   Hit and run
   Sacrifice bunt
   Off bat
3. Runner on third
4. Runners on first and third
5. Quadrant
6. No one on

Hitting Drill Rotation

1. Form swing, freeze frames
2. Tee drills
3. Toss drills
4. Short toss

DRILL 11.9.   Crack-of-Bat Drill, Part One

Purpose: To work on conditioning,
to improve baserunning skills,
to get used to picking up the third-base coach, to get used to his visual and vocal actions, and
to prepare base runners for bettering their own judgment.

Area Required: Full field.

Equipment Needed: Two fungo bats, four baseballs, and a plastic ball on a string, tied to a batting tee.

Procedure: Divide base runners into three groups.

Part one of the drill:

> One-third of base runners are at home plate.
> One-third of base runners are at first base.
> One-third of base runners are at second base.

This drill requires a regular third-base coach; a first-base coach is really not needed.

The drill begins without any baseballs at all. To start, the first player in each group takes his lead from his base. A coach holding two fungos stands at home plate and raises the bats. The runners take their secondary leads. The coach then cracks the bats together, simulating a ball being hit. The players run to the next base. The runner off second base must pay attention to the third-base coach. If the coach sends the runner home, the runner from first base continues to third base, picking up the coach. The runner from home continues to second base. If the third-base coach sends home the runner, who started at first base, the runner from home pays attention to the third-base coach. The coach has the option of doing whatever he likes: send the runner home, hold the runner, make the runner slide, stand up right on the base, and so on. After the players run, they should move to the next base (first to second, second to home, home to first), regardless of where they end up.

Points to look for: Second-base runner gets normal and secondary leads, then reacts to the crack of the bat, and reads signal from the third-base coach. First-base runner gets normal and secondary leads and reacts to the crack of the bat, reading signs from the third-base coach only if the coach is on the outfield side, behind third base. The coach's vocal and visual signs may differ according to individual systems.

The runner from second base knows that once he has passed the third-base coach, he is advancing toward home, and the third-base coach is now helping the runner from first base advance to third base or stop at second base. The runner from second base knows that if the third-base coach is down the line (in front of him) he must obey his judgment. If the third-base coach is down the line, the runner from first base finds the ball and the third-base runner. If the third-base runner advances toward home, the runner at second base makes his own best judgment. The coach can specify, prior to the crack of the bat, where the ball will be hit in the outfield.

The runner from home plate uses proper technique in getting out of the box and rounding first base while reading the base runner in front of him. (The first-base coach can help here.) The on-deck hitter/runner gives signals, such as to stand, slide and so on, to the base runner from second base on his way to score. Using the crack-of-bat drill for 10 minutes a day will provide a team with good conditioning that is sport specific.

DRILL 11.10.   Crack-of-Bat Drill, Part Two

Everything is the same as Crack-of-Bat Drill, Part One, except for the following:

The pitchers who are scheduled for long throws are put in the outfield; all other positions are filled by the remaining pitchers, managers, or graduate assistant coaches. The drill begins when the batter/runner hits the plastic ball tied on a string to a batting tee (the ball is tied on a string to keep the drill moving). Players should take a full swing, hit the plastic ball, and practice getting out of the batter's box. When the batter/runner hits the plastic ball, a coach hits a live fungo ball to the pitchers standing in the outfield. All base runners react just as they do for Crack-of-Bat, Part One.

The pitchers are not asked to throw hard, but to throw correctly as in long tossing. They may throw to any base, thus giving the runner and the third-base coach different reads.

A player's own best judgment in baseball is a very important weapon, which a coach should develop. This drill is an asset in such development. Variations can be added, such as giving signals and practicing sliding. As stated previously, this is a great conditioning drill, and it helps keep the intensity level high.

12

A NEW APPROACH TO STRENGTH
AND CONDITIONING

Some of the concepts written in this chapter may be unfamiliar to you. Therefore, we have included some of the terms in the glossary in the back of the book.

WHY CONDITION YEAR-ROUND?

A strength and conditioning program is a twofold operation. It helps to strengthen the athlete and to improve performance and reduce the chance of injury. Every strength and conditioning program encompasses the main components of fitness: strength, speed, conditioning, flexibility, and nutrition. All of this is essential in determining an athlete's complete athleticism.

Each athlete's program is sport specific because each sport places different demands on the body. Each program is split into three phases: off season, preseason, and in season. The exercises, volume, intensity, and duration are modified throughout each phase to decrease the chance of overtraining.

Testing is performed to monitor the athlete's progress. This helps determine whether any changes are needed in the program to help better the athlete. The end result of each program: athletes who are properly conditioned for competition.

A year-round strength and conditioning program is necessary for all athletes. It helps them to stay in shape year-round. It prepares them to be strong and faster than they were the previous year. Like all coaches, we want athletes to be better than they were last year. Not only does practice for skill development help, but so does strength and conditioning training. Skill training, in this case for baseball, helps the athlete become a better player.

MYTHS

In the past, strength training was frowned upon by many coaches, who thought it would make their players too bulky and cause them to lose flexibility. Others thought it was too time-consuming. As time wore on, strength training became a part of the regular routine, but only for the two months prior to in-season workouts. At that time, all weight training stopped until the season was over.

Strength training helps not only in flexibility but also, as mentioned earlier, to reduce the chance of injury. It doesn't take long to train for a sport. Throughout the year, the duration of the lifting season varies, especially in season, when travel and practice can become hectic. We talk about this later in the chapter.

BASIC MUSCLE PHYSIOLOGY

Baseball is a sport that requires repetitive short bursts of speed with a period of rest afterwards. Any activity of a start-and-stop nature is termed *anaerobic.*

There are two types of muscle fibers in our bodies: fast twitch and slow twitch. Fast-twitch muscle fibers are used during activities that require short bursts of speed (1 second to 1½ minutes). Very little, if any, oxygen is used during these activities, so they are anaerobic. Slow-twitch muscle fibers are used during activities that require long, low intense work. As the length of the activity increases, oxygen is used more as a source of energy. Such activities go without stopping for more than 2 minutes. Oxygen is readily used during these activities; thus they are called *aerobic.*

It is often suggested that an aerobic endurance program enables athletes to meet energy demands late in a competition. However, few sports go nonstop from beginning to end. Activity may be disrupted by a foul ball, a change of inning, time outs, half time, and so on. One must also consider the energy demands of each individual. Because of the demands of an anaerobic sport, an athlete cannot be expected to maintain the same metabolic intensity level throughout the game. Therefore, the length of the game may not be an appropriate way to evaluate energy needs.[1]

Specificity dictates that the mode of exercise used in training will affect the adaptations seen in the neuromuscular and metabolic systems (size and strength of the muscle, speed, endurance, and reaction time). Aerobic training affects strength and prolongs the length of training. Anaerobic training increases the body's ability to handle high lactate levels (a byproduct in the blood that reduces the muscle's chance to perform work), increase aerobic power, and enhance recovery.

Baseball is a ballistic sport, hence anaerobic. Arm actions in hitting and throwing, leg actions in base stealing, and defensive plays are all ballistic in nature. Games may take hours to play, but the individual movements are made up of quick, explosive, and reactionary movements.[2] For muscle contraction to occur, chemical energy in the form of *ATP* (adenosine triphosphate) must be readily available.[3] This helps the muscle perform the desired movement. Because ATP is in low concentration (ATP lasts only 1–10 seconds), there

---

[1]Jefferey Watts, "Sport-Specific Conditioning for Anaerobic Athletes, *NSCA Journal,* vol. 18, no. 4 (August 1996).

[2]Coop DeRenne, "Physical Demands and Biomechanical Basis for Baseball Conditioning," *NSCA Journal,* vol. 12, no. 4 (1990).

[3]J.D. MacDougall, H.A. Wenger, and J. Green II, *Physiological Testing of the Elite Athlete.* (New York: Movement Publications, Inc., 1982).

are several regulated pathways for producing it. These pathways are *creatine phosphate* splitting, *anaerobic glycosis*, and *aerobic metabolism*.

Creatine phosphate is abundant and helps produce ATP for muscle function during activity. Creatine phosphate splitting is anaerobic in nature. Because it can last for only a short period of time (10 to 30 seconds), the other pathways must become active.

Anaerobic glycosis involves the regeneration of ATP through the breakdown of carbohydrates to lactic acid. This is also an anaerobic process. Large amounts can be produced, although it is not possible to continue contraction for a long period of time. The buildup of acidosis due to the accumulation of lactic acid results in a reduction of work (30 seconds to 2 minutes).

The production of ATP through aerobic metabolism involves the breakdown of a metabolic fuel in the presence of oxygen. Oxygen is supplied to the mitochondria of the muscle cells in sufficient amounts. Therefore, aerobic metabolism requires a significant amount of time to activate the process and regenerate ATP (usually after 2 minutes of continuous work). It must be noted that all pathways work concurrently. The proportion of ATP supplied to the muscle from each process varies according to the intensity level and duration of exercise.[4]

When exercise intensity is high, it is immediately followed by an accelerated rate of ATP resynthesis from creatine phosphate stores and anaerobic glycosis. As long as the intensity of the activity is high (swinging the bat, throwing the ball, pitching), the anaerobic systems continue to supply the major source of ATP because of the inability of the aerobic system to supply enough ATP to meet the energy demands of the muscle.

The following shows the systems and their duration. Note that all systems work concurrently.

System	Duration
ATP-PC	0–10 seconds
ATP-PC, anaerobic glycosis	10–30 seconds
Anaerobic glycosis	2 seconds–2 minutes
Anaerobic glycosis, aerobic metabolism	2–3 minutes
Aerobic metabolism	3 minutes and resting

Because pitching, swinging a bat, defensive play, and so on involve short bursts of speed and high intensity, are ballistic in nature, and last only fractions of a second, we can conclude they are anaerobic in nature. The energy system responsible for the production of ATP, which allows these movements to exist, is the ATP-PC system. It is imperative that when developing a strength and conditioning program, a coach concentrate upon developing the anaerobic systems.

Let's put it into simpler terms: When a muscle is placed under stress, it must respond to that stress. In other words, it must fight against it. The muscle actually builds itself, becoming stronger and bigger to combat against that stress. The next time that stress comes,

---

[4]Jeffrey Potteiger and G. Dennis Wilson, "Training the Pitcher: A Physiological Perspective," *NSCA Journal*, vol. 11, no. 3 (1989).

the muscle is better prepared to fight against it. After a few bouts against this stress, the muscle will have become strong and big enough to handle the stress easily. For example, when an athlete bench presses 100 pounds for the first time, the muscles at work (chest, shoulders, triceps) are put under stress. They are working against a resistance (stress) that they can handle for a short period of time. Then they become fatigued. Afterward they feel sore. This is because minute tears in the muscle have formed during the work. The muscle then rebuilds itself, becoming stronger and bigger. When the time comes to bench press again, the muscles are better prepared to work against it. After a few workouts, the muscles can easily handle 100 pounds for many repetitions.

Because our muscles become strong, they can take the punishment of competition. They can take the constant twisting, turning, and pounding our bodies go through. They can combat those high forms of stress—running to first base, swinging the bat to hit the ball, throwing the ball from the outfield to home plate, or diving for a line drive. An athlete can be just as strong at the end of a game as he was when it began, with very little energy lost.

The limiting factors for performance are throwing and acceleration power, such as when running from first base to second base after a hit or stealing second base. The training objective is to link the energy systems with the limiting factors. The desired performance will be achieved when the limiting factors are not developed to the highest possible level.[5] What coaches must do is to set up a program that meets the athletes' baseball needs—one that works the anaerobic system and enhances the neuromuscular and metabolic systems. This allows gross motor adaptations from the strength and power portion of the program to be refined into more applicable sport skills during practice.[1]

STRENGTH TRAINING PRINCIPLES

The performance of exercises requires a specific number of sets and repetitions. The sets and repetitions are varied throughout the year to allow for desired gains in muscle size, strength, and power. This depends on the sport. Also, the sets and repetitions are varied to prevent overtraining. Repetitions ("reps") are the number of times an exercise is performed. Sets comprise the repetitions determined for each exercise.

Plyometrics are explosive types of exercises that help to improve speed and power. They allow the body to perform at high intensity. They also can work on power endurance when used repetitively. An example of a plyometric exercise is jumping.

Periodization is the process of varying sets, reps, and exercises throughout the year. The year is broken up into three segments: preseason, in season, and off season. During the in-season program, the goal is to maintain the strength and power gained during the off season and preseason.

The off season is usually started with an active rest period. This period may last anywhere from 2–4 weeks, determined by the coach. This period allows full recuperation, both mentally and physically, from the season. It prepares the athlete for the start of the off-season lifting and running programs.

---

[5]Tudor Bompa, *Periodization of Strength* (Toronto: Veritas Publishing Company, Inc., 1993).

The off season is a period during which an athlete can establish a base to work with, especially when the preseason nears. The athlete begins to build muscle, a process called *hypertrophy*, to prepare his body for the high-intensity bouts during the preseason and the in season. Volume is high during this period, meaning that reps are high (8–12 reps). The intensity is low. Because he is working with high reps, he needs to use low weight. Rest periods are long, lasting 1–2 minutes. The running during this period is concentrated on long–distance sprinting (800-meter or 400-meter sprint) and on improving speed mechanics. Plyometrics are performed at a low intensity. (See Tables 12.1, 12.2, 12.3, and 12.4.)

The latter part of the off-season conditioning consists of developing strength and speed. The reps are decreased to 4–6, and the intensity is higher, using heavier weights. Conditioning is geared toward shorter sprints of 20–100 yards. (See Tables 12.5 and 12.6.)

TABLE 12.1.   Baseball Summer Strength Training

Monday/Thursday

DB bench press (Dumbbell)	3×8	—	—	—	—	—	—	—	—
DB incline press	3×8	—	—	—	—	—	—	—	—
Squat	3×8	—	—	—	—	—	—	—	—
Leg extension	3×10	—	—	—	—	—	—	—	—
DB shoulder press	2×10	—	—	—	—	—	—	—	—
3-way raise	2×10	—	—	—	—	—	—	—	—
Rotator cuff circuit	1×15	—	—	—	—	—	—	—	—
Tricep extension	3×10	—	—	—	—	—	—	—	—
Sit-ups	3×35	—	—	—	—	—	—	—	—
Medicine ball:									
Sit-ups	2×20								
Rotational throws	2×20								
Russian twists	2×20								

TABLE 12.2.   Baseball Summer Strength Training

Tuesday/Friday									
Leg curl	3 × 12	__	__	__	__	__	__	__	__
Lat pulldowns (to the front)	3 × 10	__	__	__	__	__	__	__	__
Dumbbell rows	3 × 10	__	__	__	__	__	__	__	__
Upright row	3 × 10	__	__	__	__	__	__	__	__
Pullover	× 10	__	__	__	__	__	__	__	__
Barbell curl	3 × 10	__	__	__	__	__	__	__	__
Dumbbell curl	2 × 15	__	__	__	__	__	__	__	__
Forearm circuit	3 × 15	__	__	__	__	__	__	__	__

Abdominal circuit:

Hanging leg raises 10-second rest	10 reps
Hanging leg raises no rest	5 reps
Hanging knee-ups no rest	5 reps
Side crunches 10-second rest	20 reps
Sit-ups no rest	35 reps (slow, 1 rep per 2 seconds)
Crunches	15 reps (fast)

The preseason is geared to developing power and power endurance. Plyometric exercises are performed at a high intensity. Agility exercises are performed to improve coordination and quickness. Exercise intensity is very high, with reps of 2–4, volume is lower, and the duration of the exercise routines is shorter. Rest times are shortened as well. (See Tables 12.7 and 12.8.)

TABLE 12.3.   Summer Baseball Calendar

	Week 1		

Monday

Stretch	Lift	Running
(see stretch routine)		1.0-mile run

Tuesday

Stretch	Lift	Plyometrics
(see stretch routine)		All jumps 1 × 20 yards
		Broad jumps
		Diagonal broad jumps

Wednesday

Stretch
(see stretch routine)

Thursday

Stretch	Lift	Running
(see stretch routine)		1 time each drill:
		4-corner drill
		Boomerang
		3-cone drill
		Agility drill
		Dot drill

Friday

Stretch	Lift	Running
(see stretch routine)		1 × 300-yard shuttle
		within 75 sec.
		(100-yard intervals)
		2 × 60-yard sprint
		1 × 50-yard sprint

The in-season training is designed to maintain strength throughout this period. With the long season and the number of games played per week, it is often difficult to maintain strength and detraining results. Only the commitment to strength training during the in season can decrease this chance of detraining. (See Tables 12.9 and 12.10.)

Pitchers are often wary of strength training, especially during the season. With the known fact that strength can decrease when training stops, such training can be detrimental to a pitcher. Leg strength can diminish, thus decreasing leg drive in throwing. The musculature of the rotator cuff and supporting

TABLE 12.4.   Summer Baseball Calendar

	Week 2		
Monday			
	Stretch	**Lift**	**Running**
	(see stretch routine)		1.0-mile run in 8:30 min.
Tuesday			
	Stretch	**Lift**	**Plyometrics**
	(see stretch routine)		All jumps 1 × 20 yards
			Broad jumps
			Diagonal broad jumps
Wednesday			
	Stretch		
	(see stretch routine)		
Thursday			
	Stretch	**Lift**	**Running**
	(see stretch routine)		1 time each drill:
			4-corner drill
			Boomerang
			3-cone drill
			Agility drill
			Dot drill
Friday			
	Stretch	**Lift**	**Running**
	(see stretch routine)		1 × 300-yard shuttle
			within 65 sec.
			(50-yard intervals)
			2 × 60-yard sprint
			1 × 50-yard sprint

muscles of the throwing motion (back, chest, and abdominal area) atrophy or decrease in size. This can result in lower torque produced by the muscles used in throwing, thus decreasing throwing power. It can also lead to injury because the small muscles of the rotator cuff are put through tremendous stress during throwing. (See Table 12.11.)

It is important to note that any type of strength training should be supervised by a trained individual who can set up a program and teach the proper technique of all exercises. It is also important to train with a partner so that one can push the other and help spot the other. It is great for motivation.

TABLE 12.5.   Baseball Preseason Conditioning

			Week 3	
Monday				
	Stretch	**Lift**	**Plyometrics**	
			All jumps 2 × 20 yards:	Med. ball, 2 × 20:
			Broad jumps	Chest pass
			Diagonal broad jumps	Overhead throw
			Box jumps, 2 × 10:	Walkover
			Front	Clap push-ups, 2 × 15
			Side	
Tuesday				
	Stretch	**Lift**	**Running**	
			Warm-up circuit	2 sets each:
			Base running:	3-cone drill
			2 × 1st base	20-yard shuttle
			2 × 2nd base	Lunges, 2 × 15 yards
			2 × 3rd base	Ski lunges, 2 × 15 yards
			2 × home	Slides, 2 × 15 yards
Wednesday				
	Stretch			
Thursday				
	Stretch	**Lift**	**Plyometrics**	
			All jumps 2 × 20 yards:	Med. ball, 2 × 20:
			Broad jumps	Chest pass
			Diagonal broad jumps	Overhead throw
			Box jumps, 2 × 10:	Walkover
			Front	Clap push-ups, 2 × 15
			Side	
Friday				
	Stretch	**Lift**	**Running**	
			Warm-up circuit	
			Base running:	2 sets each:
			2 × 1st base	3-cone drill
			2 × 2nd base	20-yard shuttle
			2 × 3rd base	Lunges, 2 × 15 yards
			2 × home	Ski lunges, 2 × 15 yards
				Slides, 2 × 15 yards

TABLE 12.6   Baseball Preseason Conditioning

	Week 4			
Monday				
	Stretch	**Lift**	**Plyometrics**	
			All jumps 2 × 25 yards:	Med. ball, 3 × 20:
			Broad jumps	Chest pass
			Diagonal broad jumps	Overhead throw
			Box jumps, 2 × 15:	Walkover
			Front	Clap push-ups, 2 × 20
			Side	
Tuesday				
	Stretch	**Lift**	**Running**	
			Warm-up circuit	
			Base running:	3 sets each:
			3 × 1st base	3-cone drill, within 4 sec.
			3 × 2nd base	20-yard shuttle
			3 × 3rd base	Lunges, 3 × 15 yards
			3 × home	Ski lunges, 3 × 15 yards
				Slides, 3 × 15 yards
Wednesday				
	Stretch			
Thursday				
	Stretch	**Lift**	**Plyometrics**	
			All jumps 3 × 20 yards:	Med. ball, 3 × 20:
			Broad jumps	Chest pass
			Diagonal broad jumps	Overhead throw
			Box jumps, 3 × 10:	Walkover
			Front	Clap push-ups, 2 × 20
			Side	
Friday				
	Stretch	**Lift**	**Running**	
			Warm-up circuit	
			Base running:	3 sets each:
			3 × 1st base	3-cone drill, within 4 sec.
			3 × 2nd base	20-yard shuttle
			3 × 3rd base	Lunges, 3 × 15 yards
			3 × home	Ski lunges, 3 × 15 yards
				Slides, 3 × 15 yards

TABLE 12.7.   Baseball Preseason

Monday/Thursday

DB incline bench press	——	——	——	——	——	——	——	——
	——	——	——	——	——	——	——	——
	——	——	——	——	——	——	——	——
Chest fly	——	——	——	——	——	——	——	——
	——	——	——	——	——	——	——	——
	——	——	——	——	——	——	——	——
Squat	——	——	——	——	——	——	——	——
	——	——	——	——	——	——	——	——
	——	——	——	——	——	——	——	——
Step-ups	——	——	——	——	——	——	——	——
	——	——	——	——	——	——	——	——
	——	——	——	——	——	——	——	——
Rotator cuff circuit 2×10	——	——	——	——	——	——	——	——
	——	——	——	——	——	——	——	——
3-way raises	——	——	——	——	——	——	——	——
	——	——	——	——	——	——	——	——
	——	——	——	——	——	——	——	——
3-way tricep extension	——	——	——	——	——	——	——	——
	——	——	——	——	——	——	——	——
	——	——	——	——	——	——	——	——
Tricep pushdown	——	——	——	——	——	——	——	——
	——	——	——	——	——	——	——	——
	——	——	——	——	——	——	——	——
Med. ball sit-ups 3×30	——	——	——	——	——	——	——	——
	——	——	——	——	——	——	——	——
Crunches 2×40	——	——	——	——	——	——	——	——
	——	——	——	——	——	——	——	——

Sets and reps:
3×10
3×10
3×10
3×10
3×8
3×8
3×8

TABLE 12.8. Baseball Preseason

Tuesday/Friday

Leg curl	—	—	—	—	—	—	—	—
	—	—	—	—	—	—	—	—
	—	—	—	—	—	—	—	—
	—	—	—	—	—	—	—	—
Hyperextension	—	—	—	—	—	—	—	—
3 × 15	—	—	—	—	—	—	—	—
	—	—	—	—	—	—	—	—
Lat pulldown (Tuesday)	—	—	—	—	—	—	—	—
Chin-ups (Friday)	—	—	—	—	—	—	—	—
	—	—	—	—	—	—	—	—
DB row	—	—	—	—	—	—	—	—
	—	—	—	—	—	—	—	—
	—	—	—	—	—	—	—	—
Pullover	—	—	—	—	—	—	—	—
	—	—	—	—	—	—	—	—
	—	—	—	—	—	—	—	—
Chin-ups	—	—	—	—	—	—	—	—
2 × 10	—	—	—	—	—	—	—	—
DB curl or barbell curl	—	—	—	—	—	—	—	—
	—	—	—	—	—	—	—	—
	—	—	—	—	—	—	—	—
Wrist circuit	—	—	—	—	—	—	—	—
	—	—	—	—	—	—	—	—
	—	—	—	—	—	—	—	—

Wrist curl, reverse wrist curl, supination/pronation, ulnar/radial deviation, tennis ball squeeze

Side crunches	—	—	—	—	—	—	—	—
2 × 35	—	—	—	—	—	—	—	—
Med. ball rotational throw	—	—	—	—	—	—	—	—
2 × 20	—	—	—	—	—	—	—	—
Russian twist	—	—	—	—	—	—	—	—
2 × 25	—	—	—	—	—	—	—	—

Sets and reps:
   3 × 10
   3 × 10
   3 × 10
   3 × 10
   3 × 8
   3 × 8

TABLE 12.9.   Baseball In-Season Circuit-Pitchers

Name _____

Rest for 30 seconds between excercises.

Perform each exercise for 2 sets.

1. Squats	15 reps	___	___	___	___	___	___
2. Snatch squat	15 reps	___	___	___	___	___	___
3. Lunges	15 reps	___	___	___	___	___	___
4. Chest fly	15 reps	___	___	___	___	___	___
5. Dumbbell row	15 reps	___	___	___	___	___	___
6. Tricep extension	15 reps	___	___	___	___	___	___
7. Bicep curl	15 reps	___	___	___	___	___	___
8. 3-way raises	15 reps	___	___	___	___	___	___
9. Rotator cuff circuit	15 reps each	___	___	___	___	___	___
Supraspinitis, lateral raise, internal/external rotation, abduction, rhomboids, lower trap							
10. Wrist circuit	15 reps each	___	___	___	___	___	___
Wrist curl, reverse wrist curl, supination/pronation, tennis ball squeeze							
11. Med. ball sit-ups	25 reps	___	___	___	___	___	___
12. Med. ball rotational throw	15 reps	___	___	___	___	___	___
13. Med. ball overhead catch	15 reps	___	___	___	___	___	___
14. Hip raises supersetted with crunches	20 reps	___	___	___	___	___	___
15. Russian twists	25 reps	___	___	___	___	___	___

TABLE 12.10.   In-Season Circuit-Baseball

Infield/Outfield Catchers

Name _____

Rest for 30 seconds between excercises.

Perform each exercise for 2 sets.

1. Squats	10 reps	—	—	—	—	—	—
2. Leg curls	10 reps	—	—	—	—	—	—
3. Dumbbell rows	10 reps	—	—	—	—	—	—
4. 1-leg squat	10 reps	—	—	—	—	—	—
5. 3-way raises	10 reps	—	—	—	—	—	—
6. Incline bench press	10 reps	—	—	—	—	—	—
7. Wrist circuit	10 reps each	—	—	—	—	—	—
Wrist curl, reverse wrist curl, supination/pronation, tennis ball squeeze							
8. Bicep curl	10 reps	—	—	—	—	—	—
9. Tricep extension	10 reps	—	—	—	—	—	—
10. Rotator cuff circuit	10 reps each	—	—	—	—	—	—
Supraspinitis, lateral raise, internal/external rotation, abduction, rhomboids, lower trap							
11. Med. ball overhead throw	10 reps	—	—	—	—	—	—
12. Med. ball rotational throw	10 reps	—	—	—	—	—	—
13. Med. ball sit-ups	25 reps	—	—	—	—	—	—
14. Hip raises supersetted with crunches	20 reps	—	—	—	—	—	—
15. Russian twists	25 reps	—	—	—	—	—	—

TABLE 12.11.   In-Season Conditioning

Pitchers

Hollow sprints—sprint 60 yards, jog 60 yards (counts as one rep)—3 × 10, rest for 1 minute

30-yard sprints—sprint full speed, rest for 3 minutes—3 × 10

Plyometrics:

    Broad jumps—2 × 20 yards

    Power skips—2 × 20 yards

    Bounds—2 × 20 yards

    Cone jumps—2 × 20 yards

Infield/Outfield/Catchers

60-yard sprints—2 × 10

20-yard sprints—2 × 10

Game simulations—home to first, home to second, home to third, sets of 5 × 4

Plyometrics—once per week:

    Broad jumps—2 × 20 yards

    Diagonal broad jumps—2 × 20 yards

    Lateral cone jumps—2 × 10 reps

5-day pitching rotation

Day 1—pitch

Day 2—recovery (stretching)

Day 3—weight training and sprinting

Day 4—sprint training

Day 5—recovery (light stretching)

Day 6—pitch

4-day pitching rotation

Day 1—pitch

Day 2—recovery (light stretching)

Day 3—weight training and sprinting

Day 4—recovery (light stretching)

Day 5—pitch

CONCLUSION

A complete approach to strength and conditioning can develop the overall attributes associated with baseball playing. One can increase throwing power, acceleration power, bat speed, and endurance and can decrease the chance of injury. The result is a well-conditioned athlete and a better baseball player.

GLOSSARY OF TERMS

Ace   A team's best pitcher.

Aerobic   Sustained activity over a period of time, producing endurance and stamina. Describes movements that require oxygen to produce energy.

Aerobic Metabolism   A steady state of activity. Think of driving an economy car at a steady speed of 55 mph for many hours.

Agility   Ability to change direction without losing speed or balance.

Anaerobic   Explosive movement; power. Movements that do not require oxygen to produce energy.

Anaerobic Glycosis   A source of quick energy. It is very inefficient, like a high-performance car that gets poor mileage.

Appeal   The act of a fielder in claiming violation of the rules by the offensive team.

Arcing   A curved path a fielder takes toward a ground ball or fly ball.

Around the Horn   Double play; third base to second base to first base.

Astroturf   An artificial surface that replaces grass. It is like a carpet, and the ball travels much faster and takes truer bounces than it does on grass.

ATP (adrenosine triphosphate)   Chemical energy used by a muscle when it contracts.

Atrophy   Decreasing muscle size.

Backstop   A fence or wall behind home plate.

Balk   An illegal action or move by the pitcher with a runner on base, which entitles the runner to advance one base.

Ball   The baseball or a pitch outside the strike zone.

Ball Hawk   An outfielder who covers a lot of ground.

Baltimore Chop   A high bouncing ground ball.

Base   One of four points that must be touched by a runner to score a run; more usually applied to the canvas bags and the rubber home plate that mark the base points.

Base Coach   A team member in uniform stationed in the coach's box at first or third base to direct the batter and runners.

Base Line   Also called *foul line*. The white chalk line that extends from home plate through first and third bases to the outfield foul pole.

Bases Loaded   Runners on first, second, and third bases at the same time.

Base on Balls   Four pitches to a batter outside the strike zone in a single at bat, allows the hitter a free pass to first base.

Base Path   The path the runners must use when running between bases.

Bat   The object with which the batter hits the ball. It can be made of wood or aluminum.

Batter   An offensive player who takes a position in the batter's box.

Batter's Box   Where the batter must stand when ready to hit the ball.

Battery   The pitcher and catcher.

Batting Practice   Hitters' pregame practice in the batting cage on the field.

Batting Tee   An instrument that helps hitters work on swing mechanics.

Bench   Area where the teams sit during the game, usually uncovered.

Block   To stand in the path of the ball or player.

Blooper   Also called a *flair*. A weak fly ball that drops between the infielders and outfielders.

Bobble   To mishandle the ball.

Boner   A mental mistake.

Break   The start in fielding or baserunning, or the action of a pitch.

Breaking Ball   A ball that curves when thrown by the pitcher.

Bull Pen   Place where pitchers warm up and sit during the game.

Bunt   A batted ball not swung at but intentionally met with the bat and tapped slowly in front of home plate.

Can of Corn   A lazy, high fly ball that is an easy out.

Carom   The bounce a ball takes off a fence or wall.

Carry   The lift or momentum the ball takes on as it sails through the air when thrown or hit.

Catch   The act of a fielder in getting secure possession in the hand or glove of a ball in flight and firmly holding it before it touches the ground.

Catcher's Box   Box marked behind home plate where the catcher must stay.

Change of Pace   Slowly pitched ball.

Cheating   Moving closer to a base rather than playing in the fielders' normal position.

Chew Out   Yell at (admonish) a player.

Choking Up   Moving the hands up the handle of the bat to achieve better bat control.

Clean-up Hitter   The fourth hitter in the batting order.

Coach   A person appointed to perform such duties as the manager may designate.

Cocked Arm   The arm in position to throw.

Comebacker   A ball hit directly back at the pitcher.

Come Set   Going from a stand up position prior to the pitch to a ready position, anticipating that the ball will be hit to him.

Communication   Either verbal or hand signs between player and player or coach and player.

Control   The pitcher's ability to throw the ball to a specific location.

Creatine Phosphate   Analogous to the store of energy in a battery. It gets you going but soon runs out unless recharged.

Cross-back Step   A step used by an infielder to get into position to throw after fielding a ground ball to his left.

Crow hop   A quick skipping step used by a fielder to help him throw with more accuracy and momentum.

Curve   A pitch that breaks either down and away or down and in to a hitter.

Cutoff/Cutoff Man   A throw from the outfield. The infielder is the cutoff man.

Delivery   The pitcher's motion from start to finish.

Diamond   The infield area in which the bases are laid out.

Dish   Home plate.

Dive   To throw oneself head first at a ball in an attempt to catch it, or a head-first slide into a base.

Double Play   Recording two outs on one batted ball.

Downer   An overhand curve.

Drag Bunt   A type of bunt used in an attempt to get a base hit.

Dugout   Where the players sit during the game, usually covered.

Error   Misplaying a ball either batted or thrown.

Explode   To get maximum energy behind a swing or throw.

Fair Ball   Ball hit on or between the foul lines.

Fake Bunt/Slash   A faked bunt, then a swing at the pitch.

Feed   A soft toss to another fielder at a base.

Fireman   A relief pitcher.

Flair   See *blooper.*

Flat-footed   Both feet on the ground, weight back on the heels.

Flexibility   The range of motion in a joint.

Fly Ball   A ball batted in the air rather than on the ground.

Force Out   The retiring of a base runner by touching a base to which he is forced to advance. No tag of the runner is necessary.

Foul Ball   A ball that lands outside the foul line.

Four Corners   The position of the hips and shoulders in throwing. They are square to the target.

Framing   Technique used by catchers to make a pitch look like a strike.

Fungo/Fungo Bat   A ball (fungo) hit with a fungo bat. A fungo bat is a long, skinny bat used by coaches to hit ground balls and fly balls.

Gap   The space between outfielders.

Goat   The player who made the mistake that lost the game.

Gopher Ball   A home-run pitch.

Grand Slam   A home run with the bases loaded.

Grip   The manner in which a player holds a bat or ball.

Groove   Performing with a smooth effortless skill.

Ground Ball   A batted ball that bounces on the ground.

Hit and Run   Play in which the runner on first base breaks for second on the pitch and the hitter swings at the pitch to protect the runner.

Hit the Dirt   To slide or get out of the way of a pitched ball.

Hole   Space between two infielders.

Home   Home plate.

Home Run   A fair ball hit over the fence.

Home Team   The host team, which hits last in the inning.

Hop   The way the ball bounces (good hop, bad hop).

Hot Corner   Third base.

Hustle   To work or act rapidly or energetically.

Hypertrophy   Building muscle or muscle growth.

Illegal Pitch   A ball delivered when the pitcher is not in legal pitching motion.

Infield   Area containing the three bases and home plate.

Infield Fly Rule   States that the batter is automatically out when a pop fly can be easily caught by an infielder with less than two outs and runners on first and second bases or bases loaded.

Inning   A section of the game that contains six outs. Each team gets three outs in an inning. Each team gets twenty-seven outs in a game.

Intentional Walk   Results when the pitcher throws four balls intentionally to a hitter.

Interference   An action by a hitter, fielder, umpire, or fan that hinders play.

Jump Pivot   The 180-degree jump turn a fielder uses to get his body into position to throw in the opposite direction.

Keystone Sack   Second base.

Knuckle Ball   Pitch thrown by digging knuckles or fingernails into the ball. The ball floats or dances toward home plate with very little spin.

"L" Screen   Protective screen for the pitcher.

Launching Position   The position of the hands and bat when the hitter is ready to start his swing or the position of the hand when the pitcher or fielder is ready to bring the arm forward to throw.

Lead   In baserunning, the short distance a runner is off the base while the pitcher is in the set position.

Leadoff Hitter   The first hitter in the game or the first hitter in each inning.

Let Up   To throw a ball slow, not hard.

Line Drive   A ball hit on a line, not popped up in the air.

Location   The ability of a pitcher to throw the ball to the desired location.

Lunging   The premature shifting forward of the hitter's weight and hands.

Manager   The person who is responsible for the team's actions on the field, and who represents the team in communication with the umpire and opposing team.

Middle Infielders   The shortstop and second baseman.

No Hitter   Game in which a pitcher or combination of pitchers allows no hits to the opposing team during the game.

No Man's Land   A place on the field where the ball will land safely because of the fielder's indecision.

No-pump Windup   A type of windup in which the hands are not brought up over the head.

On Deck   The next hitter.

Open Toe   Used in baserunning. Pointing the front toe of the right foot at a 45-degree angle toward second base to facilitate use of the crossover step.

Overhand Delivery   Throw in which the arm is nearly vertical as the ball is released.

Passed Ball   A pitched ball that the catcher fails to stop and that permits a base runner to advance (catcher's fault).

Periodization   Process of structuring training into phases.

Pickoff   An attempt by a pitcher to retire a runner at a base.

Piggyback   One fielder backing up another fielder from about 20 feet away. Used in cut-off and relays.

Pitcher's Mound   Raised area in center of diamond from which the pitcher delivers the ball to the hitter at home plate.

Pivot   Turning of the foot and pushing against it to gain power and leverage in initial movement.

Pivot Man   The shortstop or second baseman who takes the throw at second base on the double play.

Plate Control   Ability of the hitter to reach any pitch in the strike zone. Also called *plate coverage.*

Plyometrics   Explosive types of exercises that help to improve speed and power, such as jumping rope or jumping off a box and rebounding off the ground.

Pop Fly   A ball hit high in the air in the infield.

Primary Lead   The lead taken by a base runner while the pitcher still has the ball. Usually three to four steps.

Pull Hitter   A batter who hits to the same side of the field on which he stands. A right-handed hitter pulls to left field and a left-handed hitter pulls to right field.

Punch-and-Judy Hitter   A singles hitter or one who sprays the ball to all fields.

Rabbit Ears   A player who is easily disturbed by the fans' or opposing team's comments.

Radar Gun   Used to determine the velocity of the pitch (mph).

Ready Position   The stance of a fielder when he is anticipating that the ball will be hit to him.

Relaxed Position   Used by an infielder, outfielder, or base runner when he is resting. Usually his hands are on his knees.

Relay/Relay Man   Player who passed the ball to another player.

Release Point   The point at which the ball leaves the hand of the pitcher or fielder throwing the ball.

Reliever   The pitcher who replaces another pitcher in a game.

Repetition   The number of work intervals in one set.

Rhubarb   A heated argument on the field involving the manager, umpire, and several players.

Rotation   The spin put on the baseball by the use of certain grips.

Rubber   A rectangular piece of white rubber that the pitcher's foot must be in contact with when he is ready to deliver the ball to the hitter at home plate.

Rubber Arm   A flexible arm. The pitcher who has it can throw every day.

Run Down   To chase a base runner caught between two fielders and two bases.

Rushing   Shifting the body weight forward too soon.

Sacrifice Bunt   Used when a batter must move a runner to the next base.

Sacrifice Fly   A fly ball hit to the outfield and deep enough to allow the runner on third base to tag up and score.

Safe   The status of a runner who reaches base without being tagged out by a fielder.

Screw Ball   A reverse curve.

Secondary Lead   Taken after the primary lead. It usually consists of two or three more shuffle steps toward the next base as the pitcher is about to release the ball toward home plate.

Set   The determined repetitions for each exercise.

Set Position   The pitcher's position on the rubber with runners on base.

Shading   The change of a fielder's position by a few steps to the right or left of where he ordinarily would stand.

Shagger   A player who catches thrown balls for a coach.

Shifting   Adjusting the defense to the batter or moving the feet to get into position to block a ball.

Shoe-top Catch   A ball caught off the shoe tops. Also called a shoe string catch.

Shuffle   Bringing one foot to the other without crossing the legs.

Shutout   A game in which a team does not score a run.

Sidearm Delivery   A throw in which the arm is in a horizontal position.

Signal   Movement of the hands to convey strategy to players.

Sinker   A fast ball that moves down.

Skipper   The manager.

Skip step   See *Crow hop.*

Slide   A controlled way of stopping and avoiding a tag.

Slider   A sharp, late-breaking pitch that looks like a fastball but moves just as it reaches the plate.

Slurve   A pitch that is something between a slider and a curveball. Basically it is a poorly thrown curveball.

Soft Hands   Hands that give and relax as the fielder catches the ball.

Soft Toss   A feed by one player to another player, who hits the ball into a net or fence. This drill is used to improve hitting mechanics.

Southpaw   A left-handed pitcher.

Specificity   Performing exercises that help the player meet the energy demands of a particular sport.

Spectator   A person who follows baseball with great interest. Also called a *fan.*

Square-up   The ready position of a fielder who is facing the hitter or another fielder.

Squeeze Play   A play in which the runner on third base breaks for home plate on the pitch, and the batter must bunt the ball.

Stance   The manner in which a hitter or fielder stands.

Starter   The first pitcher or a player who plays in the first inning.

Steal   A base runner's attempt to advance a base even though the batter does not get a hit or a base on balls.

Step in the Bucket   To pull away from the plate.

Stretch Position   See *Set position.*

Stride Foot   The stepping foot for throwing and hitting.

Strike Out   To swing at and miss three pitches or to take three pitches in the strike zone. Three strikes and you are out.

Strike Zone   Area from the armpits to the knees, the width of home plate (17 inches).

Sweet Spot   The good hitting area on the barrel of the bat.

Switch Hitter   A player who hits both left- and right-handed.

Tag   Touching a base runner with the ball to record an out.

Tag Up   An attempt by a runner to advance to the next base after a catch.

Texas Leaguer   See *Blooper.*

Three-quarters Delivery　The release of the ball with the arm at a 45-degree angle from the body.

Tools of Ignorance　The catcher's equipment.

Triple Play　Recording three outs on one batted ball.

Umpire　The official who calls balls and strikes at home plate and safe or out at the bases. He is the rules interpreter for the game.

Underhand Delivery　The release of the ball when the arm is below horizontal. This is sometimes called a *submarine pitch.*

Veer Out　A type of turn used in baserunning.

Visiting Team　The team that hits first in the top of the first inning.

Volume　A quantitative element of training. It involves the measuring of total work (sets × reps × load).

Walk　See *Base on balls.*

Warm-up　Pitches thrown by a pitcher before a game and between innings.

Warning Track　A dirt or gravel path just inside the outfield fence. It reminds the outfielder that he is getting close to the fence.

Whirl　To rotate or spin fast in a circular manner.

Wild Pitch　A pitched ball that the catcher cannot block and that permits a baserunner to advance (pitcher's fault).

Windup　The pitcher's position when bases are not occupied or when a runner is not likely to steal.

Zip　To throw with some pop on the ball.

Zoning　Looking for a certain pitch in a designated area of the strike zone.

INDEX